C90 0858100

D0262335

A STORY
LATELY TOLD

A STORY
LATELY TOLD

Coming of Age
in Ireland, London, and New York

ANJELICA HUSTON

**SIMON &
SCHUSTER**

London · New York · Sydney · Toronto · New Delhi

A CBS COMPANY

First published in Great Britain by Simon & Schuster UK Ltd, 2013
A CBS COMPANY

Photograph credits: page xi: Stephen Dane; page 1: Betty O'Kelly; page 3:
© Philippe Halsman Archive; pages 15, 31, 89, and 251: courtesy of the author; page
21: Florence Homolka; page 49: Toni Frissell, courtesy of the Library of Congress,
Prints & Photographs Division, Toni Frissell Collection; page 69: © Jules Buck;
pages 99 and 159: courtesy of MGM Media Licensing. SINFUL DAVEY © 1969
METROGOLDWYN-MAYER STUDIOS INC. ALL RIGHTS RESERVED;
pages 111,195, and 197: Richard Avedon, © The Richard Avedon Foundation;
page 113: Bruno Bernard, © Bernard of Hollywood/Renaissance Road Inc.;
page 131: © Jaqueth Hutchinson; page 171: © Norman Parkinson Ltd./courtesy
Norman Parkinson Archive; page 185: de Rosnay/*Vogue*, © Condé Nast;
page 215: Tim Jenkins; page 239: Bob Richardson

1 3 5 7 9 10 8 6 4 2

Simon & Schuster UK Ltd
1st Floor
222 Gray's Inn Road
London WC1X 8HB

www.simonandschuster.co.uk

Simon & Schuster Australia, Sydney
Simon & Schuster India, New Delhi

A CIP catalogue record for this book
is available from the British Library

ISBN: 978-0-85720-742-5
ISBN: 978-0-85720-743-2 (Trade Paperback)
ISBN: 978-0-85720-745-6 (ebook)

Printed and bound by CPI Group (UK) Ltd, Croydon, CR0 4YY

For Mum and Dad

One for sorrow
Two for joy
Three for a wedding
Four for a boy
Five for silver
Six for gold
Seven for a story lately told
—Traditional children's nursery
rhyme about magpies

CONTENTS

PROLOGUE

Anjelica in the yew tree at St. Clerans,
age seven

There was a shrine in my mother's bedroom when I was growing up. The built-in wardrobe had a mirror on the interior of both doors and a bureau inside, higher than I was, with an array of perfume bottles and small objects on the surface and a wall of burlap stretched above it. Pinned to the burlap was a collage of things she'd collected: pictures that she'd torn out of magazines, poems, pomander balls, a fox's tail tied with a red ribbon, a brooch I'd bought her from Woolworth's that spelled "mother" in malachite, a photograph of Siobhán McKenna as St. Joan. Standing between the glass doors, I loved to look at her possessions, the mirrors reflecting me into infinity.

I was a lonely child. My brother Tony and I were never very close, neither as children nor as adults, but I was tightly bound to him. We were forced to be together because we were on our own. Although I knew he loved me, I always felt that Tony had it in for me, a bit, and that, a year older than I, he was always having to fight for what he had. We were in the middle of the Irish countryside, in County Galway, in the west of Ireland, and we didn't see many other kids. We were tutored, and my life was mostly fantasy—wishing that I were Catholic so that I could have a Holy Communion, and wearing my mother's tutus on the front lawn, hoping a husband would come along so that I might marry him.

I also spent quite a lot of time in front of the bathroom mirror. Nearby there was a stack of books. My favorites were *The Death of Manolete* and the cartoons of Charles Addams. I would pretend to be Morticia Addams. I was drawn to her. I used to pull my eyes back and see how I'd look with slanted eyelids. I liked Sophia Loren a lot. I'd seen pictures of her, and she was my ideal of female beauty at the time. Then I would pore over the photographs of the great bullfighter Manolete, dressed in his suit of lights, praying to the Madonna for her protection, taking the cape under his arm, preparing to enter the bullring. The solemnity, the ritual of the occasion, was tangible in the pictures. Then the terrible aftermath—Manolete gored in the groin, the blood black on the sand. It mystified me that even though he obviously had won the fight, there were also photographs illustrating the subsequent slaughter of the bull. I felt it was a gross injustice, and my heart wept for both the bull and Manolete.

I found that I could make myself cry, very easily. Tony began to question whether I wasn't using this ability to my advantage. I think he had a point. But for me, it was always about feeling. People often think that looking in the mirror is about narcissism. Children look at their reflection to see who they are. And they want to see what they can do with it, how plastic they can be, if they can touch their nose with their tongue, or what it looks like when they cross their eyes. There are a lot of things to do in the mirror apart from just feasting on a sense of one's physical beauty.

PART ONE

IRELAND

Tony Veiller, Anjelica and Mindy, Ricki with Shu-Shu,
Seamus, Joan Buck, John Huston, and Tony Huston
with Moses and Flash, the Big House lawn,
St. Clerans, Whitsun, 1962

CHAPTER 1

Ricki with Anjelica,
age three months, New York City

I was born at 6:29 P.M. on July 8, 1951, at the Cedars of Lebanon Hospital, in Los Angeles. At eight pounds, thirteen ounces, I was a big, healthy baby. The news of my arrival was cabled promptly to the post office in the township of Butiaba in western Uganda. Two days later, a barefoot runner bearing a telegram finally arrived at Murchison Falls, a waterfall on the Nile, deep in the heart of the Belgian Congo, where *The African Queen* was being filmed.

My father, John Marcellus Huston, was a director renowned for his adventurous style and audacious nature. Even though it was considered foolhardy, he had persuaded not only Katharine Hepburn, an actress in her prime, but also Humphrey Bogart, who brought along his famously beautiful wife, the movie star Lauren Bacall, to share the hazardous journey. My mother, heavily pregnant, had stayed behind in Los Angeles with my one-year-old brother, Tony.

When the messenger handed the telegram to my father, he glanced at it, then put it in his pocket. Katie Hepburn exclaimed, "For God's sakes, John, what does it say?" and Dad replied, "It's a girl. Her name is Anjelica."

Dad was six feet two and long-legged, taller and stronger and with a more beautiful voice than anybody. His hair was salt-and-pepper; he had the broken nose of a boxer and a dramatic air about him. I don't remember ever seeing him run; rather, he ambled, or took long, fast strides. He walked loose-limbed and swaybacked, like an American, but dressed like an English gentleman: corduroy trousers, crisp shirts, knotted silk ties, jackets with suede elbows, tweed caps, fine custom-made leather shoes, and pajamas from Sulka with his initials on the pocket. He smelled of fresh tobacco and Guerlain's lime cologne. An omnipresent cigarette dangled from his fingers; it was almost an extension of his body. His tone was carefully unstudied and casual. His tastes were eclectic. At work he wore bush jackets and khakis, as if going to war.

Over the years, I've heard my father described as a Lothario, a drinker, a gambler, a man's man, more interested in killing big game than in making movies. It is true that he was extravagant and opinionated. But Dad was complicated, self-educated for the most part, inquisitive, and well read. Not only women but men of all ages fell in love with my father, with that strange loyalty and forbearance men reserve for one another. They were drawn to his wisdom, his humor, his magnanimous power; they considered him a lion, a leader, the pirate they wished they had the audacity to be. Although there were few who commanded his attention, Dad liked to admire other men, and he had a firm regard for artists, athletes, the titled, the very rich, and the very talented. Most of all, he loved characters, people who made him laugh and wonder about life.

Dad always said he wanted to be a painter but was never going to be great at it, which was why he became a director. He was born in Nevada, Missouri, on August 5, 1906, the only child of Rhea Gore and Walter Huston. His mother's side of the family was of English and Welsh descent. Rhea's grandfather William Richardson had been a general in the Civil War as well as attorney general of the state of Ohio, and had lost an arm at Chancellorsville. A silver sword presented to him by his regiment was later passed down to my brother Tony. William's daughter, Adelia, had married a prospector, John Gore, who started up several newspapers from Kansas to New York. A cowboy, a settler, a saloon owner, a judge, a professional gambler, and a confirmed alcoholic, he once won the town of Nevada in a poker game.

After Rhea was born, in 1881, Adelia became the editor of one of John Gore's publications, but she had already decided she would have to leave him. Sent to a convent school, Rhea consequently underwent a spiritual crisis, having made a pact with God to sacrifice her life so that her parents might continue to live together.

As a young woman, Rhea, like her parents, was drawn to

journalism. She began writing freelance newspaper articles in St. Louis and was able to obtain free passes to shows and plays as a reviewer. When a show called *The Sign of the Cross* came to town, she went backstage to interview the leading man, Wilson Barrett. She noticed someone who appeared to be an older actor, wearing a full beard and carrying a staff, but with the air of a much younger man. It was Thanksgiving a few days later when she returned to the lobby of her hotel, feeling alone in the world, and fell into conversation with a young man wearing red slippers. He told her that his name was Walter and that he was an actor. He explained that his mother had made the slippers for him, and invited Rhea to dinner. She wrote afterward, "Had it not been for a pair of red crocheted slippers, things would undoubtedly not be what they are today—their laces have tangled my life and knotted my heart strings in a way that cannot be undone."

Walter was born in Toronto in 1884, the fourth child of Elizabeth McGibbon and Robert Houghston. His family, of Scotch-Irish descent, were educators, engineers, and lawyers. Elizabeth's mother was a schoolteacher, and Robert's father, Alexander, was a pioneer who had settled in Ontario, Canada. Walter was an indifferent student, but early on displayed a passion for the variety shows at the Shea Theater. He and his best friend and older cousin, Archie, were inspired to create their own shows in the basement of Walter's house. Walter's sister, Margaret Carrington, was a gifted opera singer, credited with being the first person in America to sing Debussy.

After several attempts at conventional jobs, Walter and Archie earned enough money to enroll in acting school, then joined a traveling theater troupe. Although they rarely received a salary, they loved the life and decided to jump a boxcar on a freight train to New York. They were seventeen years old and ready to hit the big time.

Constant auditioning in New York soon paid off: both boys began to get small parts in plays, and Walter met the character actor William H. Thompson, who gave him "a whole approach to acting."

When Walter joined the touring company of *The Sign of the Cross* and performed in St. Louis, he encountered "a little girl, full of energy and everything pertaining to the arts." She didn't laugh at his slippers. Rhea was a petite five feet four, a horsewoman, a smoker, and a sports reporter. Walter and Rhea got married in secret on the last day of the year 1904, after knowing each other only a week. Rhea wore a black veil and an ill-fitting dress that she tried to cover up with her bridal bouquet for the pictures.

My father's first memory was of riding in front of his mother on a black horse over cobblestones. She loved a challenge, and Dad said she was better with animals than with people. Walter and Rhea separated when Dad was six, and he spent his early years in boarding schools. On holidays, he would travel with his father on the vaudeville circuit and with his mother to the racetracks and ballparks.

In 1917, Dad was misdiagnosed with an enlarged heart and Bright's disease, a sometimes fatal kidney ailment. Rhea moved him to the desert climate of Arizona, where he was confined to his bed for nearly two years. In that condition, unable to leave his room, he invented stories. He also had started to draw and paint, which he did for the rest of his life.

A later, more accurate diagnosis allowed Dad to escape his detention, and he moved with his mother from Arizona to Los Angeles, where he acquired a serious interest in boxing. After school, he often took a long bus ride across town to watch the matches at the Olympic Auditorium. Encouraged by a friend who shared his enthusiasm for the sport, Dad took boxing lessons at a city playground and eventually won a Lincoln Heights High School championship in his weight division and twenty-three out of twenty-five boxing-club matches. He dropped out of high school two years early, hoping to become a professional fighter, but his growing passion for writing, painting, and theater soon pulled him in other directions.

When Dad was eighteen, he reunited in New York with Walter, who was working on Broadway. Watching his father on the stage would provide him with the best education on the mechanics of acting, and enabled him to obtain a few small roles. When Dad underwent mastoid surgery that winter, Walter thought it would be best for him to go somewhere warm to recover. He gave Dad five hundred dollars and sent him to Vera Cruz, Mexico, for a couple of months. It was post-revolution, and the streets were filled with beggars and outlaws.

After taking a train to Mexico City, a journey made all the more exciting by the constant threat of ambush by bandits, Dad moved into the Hotel Genova, a former hacienda. Through its manager, a woman called Mrs. Porter, who had a glass eye and a wooden leg and wore a wig, he met Hattie Weldon, who ran the finest riding establishment in the city. Hattie introduced him to Colonel José Olimbrada, a soldier in the Mexican army who specialized in dressage. Because Dad was running short on money, Olimbrada suggested that he take an honorary position in the cavalry and have his choice of the best horses in Mexico to ride. By now he was running with a dangerous crowd, and soon Rhea arrived to persuade him to return to California, threatening that Walter would cut off the supply of money if he did not comply with her wishes.

Once talkies began in Hollywood, Walter Huston came into his own as a film actor. His first major role was opposite Gary Cooper in *The Virginian*. He would go on to become a great character actor and leading man, starring on stage and screen for the next twenty years. He portrayed Dodsworth on Broadway and appeared in the movie adaptation, in addition to acting in films such as *Abraham Lincoln, Rain, The Devil and Daniel Webster,* and *Yankee Doodle Dandy.* He had a beautiful voice and was famous for his rendition of "September Song," from the musical *Knickerbocker Holiday.*

Although Walter helped Dad get writing jobs on two films he was starring in, *A House Divided* and *Law and Order,* Dad's first few years in Hollywood were disappointing to him not only as a writer but in other ways as well. There was a marriage in 1925 to a girl he'd known in high school, Dorothy Harvey, that lasted only a year. Then in 1933 his career came to a halt when a car he was driving struck and killed a young woman who darted out into the street. Dad was absolved but traumatized, and left for Paris and London, where he became a drifter, down and out, playing harmonica for change in Hyde Park. After five years in Europe, during which he took the time to reassess his life, he returned to Hollywood, intent on making it.

In 1937 he married Lesley Black, an English girl whom he described as "a gentlewoman" in his autobiography, *An Open Book.* He divorced Black in 1946, when he was forty years old, and made Evelyn Keyes, the actress who played the sister of Scarlett O'Hara in *Gone With the Wind,* his third wife, on a spur-of-the-moment trip to Las Vegas after a vodka-fueled dinner at Romanoff's.

When the House Un-American Activities Committee (HUAC) began its intimidating interrogations in Hollywood in 1947, at the outset of the Communist witch hunts, Dad, with the writer Philip Dunne, formed the Committee for the First Amendment and, alongside a group of other well-known artists, such as Gene Kelly, Humphrey Bogart, Billy Wilder, Burt Lancaster, Judy Garland, and Edward G. Robinson, bought space in the trade papers to argue that the hearings were unconstitutional.

For several years following, many innocent people suffered as a result of having been labeled Communist supporters, even though many of them, including Dad, had never had an affiliation with the party. This experience fired his interest in working and living outside the United States.

In 1947, Dad directed Walter in *The Treasure of the Sierra Madre,* for which they both won Academy Awards.

My mother, Enrica Georgia Soma, was a ballet dancer before Tony and I were born. She was five feet eight and finely made. She had translucent skin, dark hair to her shoulders parted in the middle, and the expression of a Renaissance Madonna, a look both wise and naïve. She had a small waist, full hips and strong legs, graceful arms, delicate wrists, and beautiful hands with long, tapering fingers. To this day, my mother's face is the loveliest in my memory—her high cheekbones and wide forehead; the arc of her eyebrows over her eyes, gray-blue as slate; her mouth in repose, the lips curving in a half smile. To her friends, she was Ricki.

She was the daughter of a self-proclaimed yogi, Tony Soma, who owned an Italian restaurant called Tony's Wife on West Fifty-second Street in New York, where all of Broadway would come, including the Nelson Rockefellers, Frank Sinatra, and

Mario Lanza. Grandpa would teach them all how to sing. Ricki's mother, Angelica Fantoni, who had been an opera singer in Milan, died of pneumonia when Ricki was four. That broke Grandpa's heart. But he took a second wife, Dorothy Fraser, whom we called Nana, a pleasant, no-nonsense woman who raised my mother under a strict regime. Grandpa was dictatorial and prone to aphorisms such as "There's no intelligence without the tongue!" or "Through the knowledge of me, I wish to share my happiness with you!" When we visited, he liked to have us stand on our heads and sing "Oh, what a beautiful morning, oh, what a beautiful day." Then he would continue on with a few arias.

Tony's Wife had the warm, genteel atmosphere of Northern Italy in its dark wood, red carpeting, flocked wallpaper, and photographs of Grandpa in a bow tie posing on his head with various Hollywood luminaries. Off to the right, my uncle Nappy, in a sky-blue blazer, shaking up martinis behind the mirrored bar, bathed in a pink light. In the back of the restaurant were the kitchens, which I visited a few times with Grandpa, to see the pots boiling and the steaks sizzling, men in white shouting at one another through the steam.

The family lived upstairs in an apartment, which felt disconnected from the restaurant. It was quiet and dark with uneven carpeted floors. In the living room there was a piano with sheet music from which Nana played each morning for Grandpa to sing while he stood on his head. He claimed to have married Nana on the basis of her talent as an accompanist.

Grandpa also had a summer house, in Miller Place, a hamlet on the north shore of Long Island. Grandpa had great reverence for the foundations of the English language and spent long hours in his round blue mosaic tub meditating on a dictionary

11

in a bathroom atop his shingled two-story house, overlooking steep bluffs and the Sound below. When you ran down to the beach, the sand made an avalanche at your heels.

Philip was my mother's one full sibling. Angelica and Tony's first child, who had been called George, died as a baby. When my grandfather remarried, Dorothy gave birth to a girl and two boys—Linda, Nappy, and Fraser. Nappy was named after Napoleon, because Grandpa claimed to have Corsican blood running through his veins and thought he was a descendant of the great emperor. They all lived in the apartment above the restaurant.

Occasionally, Grandpa would have Ricki come downstairs to greet the guests, some of whom were likely to be show people—Tony's Wife had become a speakeasy for a time and had remained a favorite stopover among the Hollywood set ever since. One evening, my father walked in and was met by a beautiful fourteen-year-old girl. She told him that she wanted to be the world's finest ballerina and described how she wore out her ballet shoes, making her toes bleed. When he asked her if she went to the ballet often, she said, "Well, no," unfortunately, she couldn't. It was difficult, she explained, because she was expected to write a four-page essay for her father every time she went. So Dad said, "I'll tell you what. I'll take you to the ballet, and you won't have to write an essay. How about that?"

But Dad was called away to war. As he later told the story, quite romantically, he'd intended to hire a carriage, buy Ricki a corsage, and make it an event. Four years later, sitting at a dinner table at the producer David Selznick's house in Los Angeles, he found himself placed beside a beautiful young woman. He turned to her and introduced himself: "We haven't met. My name is John Huston." And she replied, "Oh, but we have. You stood me up once." My mother hadn't seen him since she was fourteen. Having studied under George Balanchine and danced on Broadway for Jerome Robbins, Mum had been the youngest member to join the best dance company in the nation, Ballet Theatre, which later became American Ballet Theatre. Now, at eighteen, she was under contract to David Selznick, and her photograph had been published on the June 9, 1947, cover of *Life* magazine. Philippe Halsman had come to photograph the company's prima ballerina but had chosen to take my mother's picture instead. In the photo spread inside the magazine, she was likened to the *Mona Lisa*—they shared that secret smile.

CHAPTER 2

Anjelica and Tony with Ricki, Long Island, 1951

My mother got pregnant with Tony when she was eighteen and my father was in his mid-forties. She'd obviously fallen deeply in love with Dad, and sacrificed a future career for him. He took her across the border to Mexico on February 10, 1950, got a divorce from Evelyn Keyes, and had a justice of the peace marry him and Mum that same night in La Paz, Baja. Billy Pearson, an art collector and one of the leading jockeys in the United States, was their best man. He had offered to ride Dad's filly, Bargain Lass, at Santa Anita, in exchange for a piece of pre-Columbian art if he won the race, which he did. This was the start of their lifelong friendship—a mismatched physical sight gag, they were the tall and the short of it, with Dad towering above the agile, diminutive Billy.

An article from Monday, March 20, 1950, in the *Los Angeles Times* under the headline "Director Confirms His Marriage to Starlet," read:

Offhand, he can't remember the date of the ceremony, but John Huston, Academy Award winning film director, today confirmed the rumor that he has been secretly married for some time to Ricki Soma, film starlet and former model, whose enigmatic smile caused her to be dubbed "The Mona Lisa Girl." The wedding, Huston declared, took place in La Paz, immediately following his February 10 divorce to Evelyn Keyes in Mexico. "Ricki and I started going together during the period of my separation from Evelyn," the director said. "But I believe I met her when she was a little girl at her father's restaurant on Fifty-second Street in New York."

According to Huston, his wife is spending a few days at the mountain home of his father, Walter Huston. Asked if he and his bride planned a honeymoon, now that the secret's out, the director laughed and said, "No, I have given up those things." It was his fourth marriage.

Tony was born on April 16, 1950, nine days after the death of our grandfather Walter Huston. Fifteen months later, my mother had me and went into a serious postpartum depression. I'm sure she was desperately lonely for my father. Nana and Grandpa offered to look after Tony and me on Long Island, in order to allow Mum to travel to London to be with Dad, who was in post-production on *The African Queen*. I was six weeks old and Tony was still in diapers when Mum flew us from L.A. to New York to stay with the Somas. Then she left to join Dad in Paris, where he was now in pre-production for *Moulin Rouge.* I was covered from head to toe with a terrible rash. I had been crying between feedings, so the pediatrician in California had prescribed phenobarbital. They had basically been doping me to keep me quiet. Nana put me on baby formula and soon I was flourishing.

Mum returned several months later to take Tony and me to France. From what I understand, Dad was causing her a lot of anxiety. The situation was particularly difficult for my mother, because Dad would not allow her to stay in Paris and had packed her off to a castle in Chantilly with us children. She must have resented our whining, greedy, egotistical little selves, so hungry for her attention. She wrote to Nana that Dad was "tired" and the children "exhausting." She complained that John "has pulled his preproduction trick, and just stays there all the time while I cart his laundry back and forth." But she warned, "He's about to get screwed though, because I have ordered a suit from Schiaparelli, bought another suit on sale at Dior, and am about to buy out Balenciaga, who I think makes the most wonderful coats and dresses in the world. Also ordered some hats, and if I don't turn out to be the cat's pajamas when I get through, it won't be my fault."

She went on to say that the screenwriter Tony Veiller's wife, Grace, had told her that her husband thought Mum was the "only person to play the part of Myriamme Hayim" in Dad's next film, *Moulin Rouge,* and that the girls they'd tested so far had all turned out wrong. Mum was "concentrating quietly on the natural law that says if you want something hard enough, you'll get it." She hoped they would allow her to test. But she thought "Dear John is subconsciously against it, because despite suggestions from every quarter, he says, 'Oh no.' "

Mum did not think he felt brave enough to put his wife in one of his pictures. Obviously not. Within a few weeks, he had cast the film and was making love to the woman set to play Myriamme—Suzanne Flon, a popular stage actress with the Comédie-Française. This liaison, which was to become a life-long affair, must have hit Mum terribly hard. She had given birth to two babies in under two years, and already Dad had moved on.

In a letter to Nana, she confided how he indulged Tony for only a few minutes and then asked her to take him away. She described Tony and me as "wretched today. Tony trying to cut his two bottom teeth or whatever they are, and in addition to that, has an awful cold. Anjelica suffers from diarrhea frequently now that she's cutting teeth right and left. Thanks so much for the rubber pants." She must have been in hell. Over the summer Dad rented us a farmhouse in Deauville, on the northern coast of France.

In her letters to Grandpa, Mum expressed a wish to join a repertory company, or to see if there might be auditions at the Windsor Playhouse in New York. It must have been very frustrating, in view of her training as a dancer, her ambition and her discipline, and all she had left behind when she married Dad. I cannot but imagine that she had dreams of being his muse; and even though she affectionately described Tony's and my first utterances, and seemed to derive joy from us, there was also a note of exasperation at having found herself made something of a prisoner by her exhausting, if adorable, children. I am sure she felt let down by circumstance.

In a white silk moiré baby book, its cover hand-painted with the image of a smiling baby sucking on her toes, my mother diligently recorded the first facts of my existence: First smile at four weeks. First walk (five steps) at thirteen months, two weeks. First words, "Bye-bye."

CHAPTER 3

Anjelica, Ricki, and Tony, 1956

My first memories are of Ireland. Dad moved us there in 1953. He had visited Ireland two years earlier, in 1951, before I was born. He'd been invited by Oonagh, Lady Oranmore and Browne, to stay at her house, Luggala, and attend a hunt ball in Dublin at the Gresham Hotel. Dad had watched as the members of the legendary Galway Blazers played a game of follow-the-leader that involved angry waiters swinging champagne buckets, and young men leaping off a balcony onto the dining tables, as the music played on into the night and the whiskey flowed. Dad had said that he expected someone would be killed before the ball was over. In the days following, he fell in love with the scenic beauty of the country.

I remember being in bed at Courtown House—a tall, gray stone Victorian manor that Mum and Dad were renting, in Co. Kildare. Mum came into my room, wrapped me in a blanket, and carried me downstairs. The house was dark and silent. Outside on the front steps in the frosted night, Dad held Tony in his arms. The sky was raining meteors. I remember Mum saying, "If you make a wish, it will come true," and together, the four of us watched the mysterious passage of dying stars fading through the firmament.

Tony and I were given rocking horses at Christmas. At least his rocked—it was dark, dappled gray, had a red patent-leather saddle and bridle, and plunged back on its base like a bucking bronco. My horse was heavy, mottled brown, made of painted tin. It humped up and down according to the pressure applied to its foot pedals, and groaned like something in pain. I found the disparity between them highly irritating and cried pitifully when Tony refused to let me up on his, even for a few minutes.

The famous combat photographer Robert Capa came to Courtown and was one of the first to take pictures of Tony and me as toddlers, crawling on a polished wood floor, wide-eyed, like two little birds that had fallen out of their nest.

Tony and I would sit on the upstairs landing at the top of the long quadrangle staircase of Courtown House and watch Dad at work from above, as he stalked slowly back and forth on the black-and-white inlaid marble squares that paved the hallway. This was a serious process. His secretary, Lorrie Sherwood, told us he was writing and never to interrupt.

Early on, we were warned that certain things should by no means be touched. One such item was an automatic clothes wringer, a contraption screwed atop the washing machine, consisting of two porcelain rollers that squeezed the last drops of water from washed clothes before they were hung on the line. I have no idea why this object held me in a seductive thrall, but the attempt I made to send a towel through it one morning when backs were turned ended traumatically with my entire arm mashed up to the armpit between the wringers. Likewise, an attempt to rescue a daisy before the lawn mower got there resulted in losing a chunk of my little finger.

Once in a while, the adults would agree to play us the score of *Peter and the Wolf,* which I found both thrilling and terrifying, and from which we invariably ran away screaming to hide in the nursery. There was a frightening book called *Struwwelpeter*—a German cautionary story about a child who sucked his thumb and had all his fingers cut off by a tailor, which included a horrible illustration of the poor boy, his hair standing on end, bleeding profusely from his severed digits. This alarmed me, because I was a confirmed thumb-sucker, although I noticed a certain grim amusement my parents seemed to derive from the book, and I guessed I would be spared the tailor's pinking shears.

Tony and I were fed breakfast in the nursery. Molly, a member of the kitchen staff, tall and lank, with the hint of a dark mustache, served us cold porridge floating in milk. I had a loathing for milk, even the way it looked in the bottle, opaque and thick with a blue tint at the edge of the glass—my diaphragm constricted at the sight of it. My place mat had illustrations from the rhyme "Mary Had a Little Lamb." I knew what the words meant, and I would read the text over and over as I waited to be released from the table. For some unknown reason, it was considered appropriate to present children with foods they hated and then to keep them prisoner until they ate.

In a corridor next to the dining room stood the highly sophisticated dollhouse that belonged to our landlord's daughter, which I was forbidden to touch. I would peer through its perfectly curtained windows, marveling at the world in miniature—the tiny grand piano, the little stuffed armchairs. I dreamed of being a fairy and taking up residence inside.

When I was three, Kathleen Shine came to look after us. With a small, tidy frame, calm blue eyes, short frizzy brown hair, and high cheekbones, she looked very much like Katharine Hepburn. She was modest, tolerant, gentle, and firm— sort of like Mary Poppins without the umbrella, and Irish. She wore the high starched collars and light-cotton denim dresses that she had worn at her former job, looking after babies in a Dublin hospital. When Mum asked her how she wanted to be addressed, she replied simply, "Nurse." She was as fair and kind as any soul I've ever met, and Tony and I adored her. Nurse was a steadying force throughout our childhood and devoted herself selflessly to us. Above all, she was dedicated to Mum.

I remember Betty O'Kelly coming into my room to say good night and asking if I could fasten the little crystal-cut buttons at the nape of her pale lemon silk blouse. She had been a debutante, a well-born Anglo-Irish girl, cheerful and innocent. Now in her late twenties, she was sportive, fun, pretty, and an exceptionally fine horsewoman. She lived in the nearby village of Kilcullen with her family and had taken to riding over to Courtown House with some regularity; she had befriended my parents and introduced them to the local gentry and to the members of the Kildare Hunt Club. My father had great regard for women on horseback. The sight of Betty mounted on a fine Irish mare must have enchanted him. "Betts," as we came to know her, had an intrepid spirit. She had driven an ambulance for the Wrens, the Women's Royal Naval Service, during the Second World War and could change a tire in ten minutes, which was a good thing if you were ever stranded out in the bogs with her.

It was Betty who brought Paddy Lynch, an ex-jockey, to work as a groom for Dad's horses, and he remained with us for the following twenty years. Small in stature, Paddy was fine-boned with blue eyes and clear brown skin, and he always wore a tweed jacket, glasses, and a cloth cap.

In the fall, we would go with Paddy into the woods to plug up foxholes; if the cubs were shut out of their dens, there would be more to chase when they were homeless in hunting season. We had a beautiful little pony trap—a varnished two-wheeler that moved along at a pretty fast clip. I loved being bundled up in blankets on Mum's lap, watching Betts wield the reins and crack the whip. In the winter, I wore a green snowsuit, a hand-me-down from Tony. I hated the look and feel of it when it was zipped up tight to my chin. It made me claustrophobic.

Betts taught Tony and me how to make an apple-pie bed, with the sheet folded back on itself halfway, as a practical joke, so the victim could not get into bed. And when Dad's friend and producer Ray Stark came to stay, she showed us how to place and activate an electric razor between the sheets so as to terrify him during the night.

Another visitor was Count Friedrich von Ledebur, a member of the Austrian cavalry and a legendary horseman, who was married to Iris Tree, the daughter of Sir Herbert Beerbohm Tree. Friedrich was even taller than Dad and had piercing eyes in a sharply defined, aristocratic face. Dad had cast him as Queequeg in *Moby Dick*. I was afraid of him. He reminded me of a lion. It was obvious that Dad loved him and had great respect for him.

Dalton Trumbo, the blacklisted writer, also stayed at Courtown. He was a kind man, a sweet soul. It seems to me that of my father's friends, the ones who were writers were more understanding, more interested, more engaged than the rest.

We rode ponies early. I was given Honeymoon when I was four. She was very old and expired under me mysteriously as I was cantering her around a field. One morning, walking with Nurse, we were surprised when Tony came out of the woods riding his pony, Paddy Lynch holding the lead rein. When the animal saw us, he suddenly reared up and bolted. Paddy lost hold of the halter and Tony fell. We watched in horror as his foot caught in the stirrup and he was dragged, his head bouncing on the gravel, all the way up the driveway. When the pony came to a shivering halt outside the front doors of the house, my parents rushed out and disengaged Tony from the saddle. He had to go to the hospital in Dublin. Mum told me they didn't know how bad it was; he was pretty much scraped bald. I made a plaster cast from a mold of one of the seven dwarfs, painted and varnished it with Nurse, and took it to him on a visit there. Tony's head was wrapped in bandages. I remember feeling separate and distant from him at the hospital, because it was a place that I didn't know, and it scared me. He was on another level. This big thing had happened to him. It set him apart.

Betty had bought Waterford, a hunter, for Mum in a sale. She was a coffin head, a tall dull-bay mare with a mind of her own. Mum made valiant efforts to impress Dad, but she got dumped practically every time they rode out. She made forays into the hunting field, always immaculately dressed, with a bowler hat on her head and her ballet toes pointed outward. At the first wall she and Waterford came across, the horse would refuse, and Mum would come tumbling down. She broke her wrist in one fall. But as Dad later told the story, one day, stunningly, Waterford cleared all the jumps. My mother had lasted through the hunt. It was a triumph. The fifty-odd riders were clattering back down the boreens, the back roads, until they came to a farm and somebody opened a gate to a pigsty. All of a sudden, Dad looked to the left and saw that Waterford was slowly plunging her feet back and forth in the muck. He said, "Ricki. Pull her up!" But of course, it was too late. Waterford went down. All the way. And started to roll. My mother disappeared momentarily from view. When she stood up, she was covered in pig shit from head to toe, nothing visible but her eyes. That was the last time Mum ever hunted.

We were in a plane, flying over turquoise water, on our way to visit Dad in Tobago, where he was filming *Heaven Knows, Mister Allison.* His home there was a two-story house that stood alone on a pale gold beach, with high palm trees all around that the native boys climbed to cut down coconuts. In the mornings we awakened to the smell of bacon frying on an open barbecue. Every Saturday evening outside the house, a party would gather to cook crab stew in a giant pot and dance the limbo deep into the night, to the rhythm of the island steel drums. Tony and I would dance with them by the firelight and try to pass under the stick without making it fall. I remember an electric eel of a woman who somehow managed to get under no matter how far they lowered it, and everybody would be laughing and singing, their teeth white in the darkness. The air at night was full of fireflies and the same temperature as your skin.

One morning while we were swimming, it started to rain, a soft shower on a warm sea. When we walked onto the beach, I saw something shining, like painted leopard skin, and pulled a large perfect cowrie shell out of the sand. I got a terrible sun-burn in the first week; my milk-white skin was scalded and coming off in ribbons. Dad put me in an ice-cold shower and I screamed with pain.

A movie starring Deborah Kerr was screened in a theater. Deborah, whom Tony and I had christened "Mrs. Boogum," and Bob Mitchum were there. Beside their seats on the aisle were tall stand-up placards with their names spelled out in big black letters. She was in a silvery blue dress with her hair up, radiant, like a princess, and everyone was deferential to her. Mitchum was as tall as Dad, deadpan, with dark wavy hair and a pronounced cleft in his chin. They were joking and seemed to be on good terms. Before the movie started, all three stood up and everyone clapped. This was my first taste of what fame looked like.

One night, Dad took us through the jungle to a big, open building, like a barn. It seemed we were the only white peo-ple there. On a raised, ringed-off platform at the center of the floor, two men were boxing. Someone asked Dad to ref-eree the next match. Leaving his seat beside me, he climbed under the ropes into the ring. At a distance in the dark heat, he was a stick figure in a white linen suit, prowling and bobbing between the fighters.

Dad had a pet agouti, a rabbit-like creature with grizzled fur and an extraordinary capacity for speed. He fed it coconut and raisins at breakfast and said it was the fastest animal in the world, but I never saw it in full gallop. Down at the harbor they had caught the sea turtle that was to take Mitchum for an underwa-ter ride in the movie. It was an enormous creature, with a great shell from under which a vulnerable-looking head was poking. There was a boat that took you out to the reefs, and they gave you a glass tray to look down into a wild aquarium—an amazing wealth of fish and other sea creatures populated these waters.

There was a costume party at the hotel one night. Tony went as a clown, in a striped shirt and Dad's big shoes; it was what he wanted to be when he grew up. Mum made me a little tutu, with sequins sewn on a pink satin bodice, and layer upon layer of pink and yellow tulle. I thought it was so beautiful, I never wanted to take it off.

CHAPTER 4

Aerial view of the Big House, St. Clerans

I was five when we moved from Courtown House to St. Clerans, a 110-acre estate in Craughwell, Co. Galway. Some twenty miles in from the coast, the West Country looked as if the sea had recently washed over it—the hawthorn trees on the high embankments turned their shoulders from the wind. On the boreens that intersected the potato fields, high wet grass and Queen Anne's lace bordered the bog lands, pastures, and coverts off the Dublin-to-Galway road. Three miles before Craughwell, down a shadowy green avenue of high elms and chestnut trees, the passage through a stone gateway led to a generous courtyard with a limestone, slate-roofed two-story cottage on the left, the Little House. A round lawn occupied the center of the courtyard, where a painted cast-iron Punchinello, wearing a tricorn hat and grinning a gap-toothed smile, perched cross-legged on a column, fanning himself. He was Dad's newest import from France.

The Little House was the steward's house to my father's future home, the Big House—just a few hundred yards away, across a bridge over a trout stream with a little island and a gentle waterfall, where a great gray heron pecked hatchlings from the shallows on one leg. When their new friends from Galway, Derek and Pat Le Poer Trench, first brought my parents to see St. Clerans, the seventeen-room estate was in disrepair. Dad purchased the property from the Land Commission for ten thousand pounds. For the next four years, my mother worked on restoring the houses. They were united in this endeavor.

Opposite the Little House were the stables, and above them, Dad's painting loft, where he would live temporarily until the Big House was completed. The loft had sea-grass matting on the floors and bull's-eye windows with seats of white báinín wool. In the bedroom, the walls were, in Mum's words, "red, the color of a Galway petticoat." A Galway petticoat was a heavy skirt made from lamb's wool and vegetable-dyed. When we were first in Ireland, they were sometimes, if rarely, seen on the women up in Connemara and those living out farther on the Aran Islands. If the wearer was a widow, a black grosgrain ribbon would circle the hem; if she had lost children, there would be additional circles of ribbon. Driving with Mum on a deserted stretch of road between Maam Cross and Ballynahinch, we once saw an old lady under a black shawl with five black rings sewn to the hem of her petticoat.

Next door was the groom's house, which Paddy and Breda Lynch came to occupy with their children—Mary, almost a year younger than I was, with black hair and bright blue eyes, whom I played with, and Patsy, who was Tony's sidekick.

The Little House was where Mum, Nurse, Tony, and I lived. The rooms were comfortable and cozy, the hall under the stairs was hung with hats, and two orange Sheffield porcelain dogs sat atop a side table in the entryway. The sitting room, with its salmon walls, green carpet, and brown silk curtains looking onto the garden, had a huge stone fireplace.

There was a fine selection of records at the Little House. My mother favored Edith Piaf, Charles Aznavour, Ella Fitzgerald, Yves Montand, Frank Sinatra, Billie Holiday; there was an eclectic collection of folk, country, and Calypso albums, including Lead Belly, John Jacob Niles, the Kingston Trio, Burl Ives, Marty Robbins, and Harry Belafonte. We listened to a Frenchman called Mouloudji, who sang a song, "Comme un p'tit coquelicot," about a girl who is shot by her jealous lover in a field of poppies, and to Count John McCormack, the Dubliners, and Brendan O'Dowda. There were also spoken-word records—among them, Marlon Brando in *Julius Caesar,* Laurence Olivier as Hamlet, and Walter Huston's reading of *The Gettysburg Address,* as well as comedy albums such as *Bawdy Songs and Backroom Ballads,* by Stan Freberg, and the great recordings of Mike Nichols and Elaine May.

At the end of the short hall was the garden room, with shelves containing row upon row of Penguin paperbacks and back issues of *The New Yorker.* The wallpaper was a crisscross pattern of bamboo and ivy on a white background. To the left of the hall was the kitchen, with a round table and a lazy Susan by the double windows overlooking the courtyard.

Upstairs was Mum's room, with wallpaper of fig leaves on a pale blue background. The windows looked out over a giant yew in a walled garden filled with exotic trees and shrubs that its former master, an explorer named Robert O'Hara Burke, had brought back from his world travels during the mid-nineteenth century. On Mum's bedside table was, as she described it, "a pale green jade horse's head, that curves swanlike to form something resembling a sword handle."

Mum's evening dresses were couture, somehow too glamorous for Ireland. She was very chic and had a real sense of humor about the way she dressed. She'd buy tweed in Clifden or Donegal, take it over to Paris, and have Chanel make it up into suits. At a time when no one else in Ireland wore blue jeans, she did. She wore ruffled Spanish shirts, a gondolier's hat with a red ribbon, and a gold bracelet with a medal of the Madonna of Guadalupe—a fixture on her wrist, which she'd been given by dignitaries in Cuba when she went there as a ballet dancer. She wore a gold ring with a little leopard climbing over a bush of diamonds. One day she showed me a collection of the most beautiful jeweled hats from Dior. Already they seemed like relics from her former life, along with the hamper of tutus and tulle she kept for me for "dress-up."

The guest room was next door to Mum's. Two primitive eighteenth-century paintings, one of an outsized cow and another of an enormously distended sheep, hung on either side of a French wrought-iron bed.

Tony and I shared the front bedroom overlooking the courtyard. Mum had decorated it like the interior of a circus tent: gray-and-white-striped wallpaper, with painted papier-mâché animals that Dad had brought back from India, lining the shelves alongside Mum's old ballet books—*Flight of the Swan: A Memory of Anna Pavlova; Nijinsky;* a book of cartoons of the ballet dancers Michel Fokine, Alicia Alonso, and Tamara Toumanova—next to my favorites, *The Little Prince, Orlando, Alice in Wonderland, Babar,* and *Madeline.* Our beds were French antique candy-striped four-posters, Tony's blue, mine pink, with a white organza frill on top. At night Tony would sing and pound his face into his pillow, which made it hard for me to get to sleep.

Outside, the vegetable garden grew stoutly under the green thumb of Odie Spellman, the head gardener. Odie was in his eighties when we came to St. Clerans. He told me that one day the wind had lifted him and his umbrella several miles in a storm, all the way to Carabane. Mary and I fully believed him. Tony, Patsy, Mary, and I would run behind the stables through the black wrought-iron gates bordered on either side by fuchsia bushes, up the path into the vegetable beds, grazing as we went on Brussels sprouts, cabbage stalks, tiny peas fresh from their pods, prickly gooseberries, red and black currants dangling on the vine, and the occasional fat pink strawberry. Mum encouraged me to have my own garden, and I planted nasturtiums, in the shape of a heart, like I'd seen from the train traveling from Davos to Klosters in Switzerland.

There was the shell of a Norman castle that dated from 1308, but it was kept under lock and key by an inheritor, Mrs. Cole, who came to visit it yearly but would never sell it to my father for fear he would tear it down. This, of course, would have been unthinkable to him. Not that it made any difference to Patsy, Mary, Tony, and me; we climbed easily over the wall and spent many happy hours running up and down its circular staircase of ancient polished stone and playing in the ruins.

In the long summer evenings when it would stay light past our bedtime, we would have endless games of tick, the Irish version of tag. Later, when we had visitors from England and America, children of our parents' friends, we learned how to play Sardines, a version of hide-and-seek, and often dressed up to amuse ourselves or, if in luck, a passing adult.

I spent a lot of time in veils and loved to dress up. I remember running back and forth with Tony, in and out of our bedroom at the Little House, putting on outfits to make our parents laugh. After exhausting several different efforts from the dress-up hamper, I charged into the bathroom naked and sprinkled talcum powder on my ass. I ran back into Mum's bedroom, turned around, exposing my bare bottom, and declared, "I'm Japanese." And this, for some reason, got a gale of laughter. I remember feeling extraordinary satisfaction at that early applause, and to see Mum and Dad briefly united in mirth was like winning a prize.

To celebrate our arrival in the West, we were invited by the parish to a dance in the church hall at Carabane, some three miles from St. Clerans. I wore a blue tartan dress that had belonged to Grandma Angelica at the turn of the century. The room was dark, with wooden floors and tall windows, and it smelled of damp and porter. Girls on one side of the hall, men on the other. Dad lifted me onto his shoulders and walked me around above the heads of the dancers; I could feel his pride in me, his pleasure in showing me off to the crowd.

Dad called Tony "my son and heir," and it was generally expressed to us that one day Tony would inherit St. Clerans. I think we were, if unconsciously, already vying for the attention of our parents. Tony complained that I was spoiled, that I got my way all the time. And I think he was jealous of the attention I drew because I was a bit more nimble than he was. I knew how to play people. I was romantic and companionable and a bit of a crybaby. But I also knew how to make people laugh, and I had an ease that he didn't seem to possess.

One day, Tony organized a boxing match between a local boy and me on the front lawn of the Little House. A single blow to my mouth from his fist and my two front baby teeth went flying. Dad, who was in Japan making *The Barbarian and the Geisha,* volunteered to get me a perfect pearl to fill the gap. This started a ritual in which he would give me a precious stone every year. A ruby when I had the measles "to match my largest spot," an emerald for Christmastime in Ireland, a single canary diamond because every girl should have one. Tony in turn received an antique orrery and a carved cherrywood crossbow from the court of Louis XIV.

> *Dear Santa,*
> *Please*
> *may I have a baby*
> *in a cradle*
> *with a pink bow*
> *on it and a box*
> *of sweets and*
> *a little book*
> *I would also*
> *like a necklace*
> *and a bracelet*
> *and earrings*
> *a doll's house*
> *and some perfume*
> *and a bigger fairy dress*
>   *Love, Anjelica*

I wrote this letter one Christmas Eve under great duress in front of a big turf fire in the Little House sitting room. I remember breaking down several times: the difficulty of getting my letters straight, desiring all those presents, and the exhaustion of having to spell it all out on paper. It was the year before Tony blew the whistle on Santa Claus.

On Christmas morning, we awoke at the crack of dawn after a fitful sleep following every attempt to stay awake and catch Santa in the act. We dove to the end of our four-poster beds to check out the stockings we'd hung the night before, complaining about the lumpy fillers, the walnuts and foil-wrapped tangerines, burrowing deep for what often proved to be the best presents of the year: a charm bracelet with a miniature enameled Jonah praying inside the mouth of a golden whale, a tiny Etruscan ring with the black cameo of an angel. Each individually wrapped by Mum.

On Boxing Day (St. Stephen's Day), the Wren Boys, or Mummers, would come to St. Clerans wearing crude masks, lace curtains, and their mother's lipstick. Their song went:

The wren, the wren,
The king of all birds,
St. Stephen's Day
Was caught in the furze.
Although he was small,
His courage was great,
Cheer up, old woman,
And give us a treat!

At this point, they'd give you a glimpse of the tortured little bird they were carrying in a cardboard box. Mum always bought the birds from them, and we'd try to feed them worms, but they were usually too traumatized to live, and we'd have a sad little burial in the garden before the first day of the year.

I remember a pine tree lit up with colored bulbs in the garden room, hearing Tony's and my new budgies chirping in their cage, and folding my arms, leaning over to slide down the banister on my armpits, then realizing that I'd tilted too far, falling over the rail, and dropping onto my head, maybe ten feet, to the floor below. As I came to, Dad was holding me on his lap. "Get her some sherry, honey," he said to Mum. It tasted delicious as I sipped it, lying in my father's arms, feeling dizzy. I loved the Little House. It was intimate.

Mum would give me jobs for a few shillings an hour, like digging in the lawn with a potato peeler for dandelions to make salad, or polishing the silverware. Every day I was expected to make my bed with the hospital corners favored by Nurse. I had to shine my own shoes and, as soon as I could be trusted not to burn myself, to iron my shirts. Mum said you had to be able to do these things in case you grew up to be poor and couldn't have servants.

As a child, she herself had to make many beds and change the water in many vases and do the washing up. I understood, and although it was tedious, it made basic sense. What I didn't understand was that the same did not seem to apply to the boys, or, more specifically, to Tony, whose only appearance at the kitchen sink was to gut trout or dismember small birds.

My first perfume was Blue Grass. I loved the bottle, with the flying turquoise horse with flowers in its mane. Then Mum gave me Diorissimo, which smelled like lily of the valley. Mum wore Chanel No. 5, and later, Guerlain's Shalimar, which was exotic and spicy, like burnt vanilla. But each year, when Nan Sunderland would make her appearance from America, the all-encompassing odor of Mary Chess Carnation permeated the ether and lingered for weeks in the Little House after she had gone. Nan was Walter's widow; we called her "Gran," though she wasn't much older than Dad. She was a tall redhead with heavily freckled skin, who wore beaded hairnets and trousers cut high at the waist and wide at the hips, tapering above white ankle socks and penny loafers. She also wore a sizable Bengal ruby on her wedding finger, which I later inherited.

At that time, having converted to Christian Science, she had decided not to accept presents at Christmas. This outraged Tony and me; we were adamant that she should accept our offerings, and left our gifts piled outside her door for her to step over whenever she left the room, until we were told by Mum not to annoy her, that she was fragile.

As far as I reckoned, Nan had the resilience of a sequoia. She had great affection for Dad and would swoop to him, wrapping her arms about his neck, reciting snatches of poetry, or whispering in his ear. Later, when Dad moved to the Big House, she stayed up there, drifting about in a negligee of powder-blue satin, perched at the bay window on the upper landing, alongside the Greek marble horse's head, reciting lines from *Playboy of the Western World*. She had been a stage and radio actress and had met Walter in 1928 when they were both performing on Broadway in *Elmer the Great* at the Lyceum Theatre. She was his third wife, following Rhea Gore and Bayonne Whipple, with whom he had partnered in vaudeville during the early twenties.

Tony and I were homeschooled, first by a pale redheaded Frenchman with a short temper called Monsieur Monquit.

Gazing into a hand mirror during our lessons, he would trim his thin ginger mustache with small gold scissors. I successfully charmed him into allowing me to do pretty much anything I wanted. It worked particularly well if I spoke in a baby voice.

Margot Stewart was our first governess—she had been secretary to the cultural attaché at the French embassy in London. Idelette followed Margot; she was French and pretty and wore angora sweaters and headbands. She had a vast collection of glass and porcelain miniatures, which Tony tossed into the mossy undergrowth beneath the giant branches of the yew tree in the garden. Idelette was followed by Leslie Waddington, whose father, Louis, a friend of Mum's, owned the Waddington Art Galleries on Cork Street in London. I found Leslie a lot harder to charm than Monsieur Monquit. He had dark curly hair, fair skin, arched eyebrows, an aquiline nose, and a narrow mouth. He was erudite, a big reader of Proust. He was one of those people who seem like seniors before their time, with an air of forbearance. Leslie was very visual—he liked to show us flash cards of the Old Masters. In my first art lesson, he demonstrated the effects of light and shadow on an egg. But he was rigid when it came to multiplication tables.

At six I was dreamy and had difficulty concentrating. Mum wrote to Dad in Japan, where he was filming *The Barbarian and the Geisha,* "Anjel, of course, is pure artist. Everything comes from intuition, some deep incontrovertible source knows all."

Because I spent long periods of time in front of the mirror, Leslie commented that I was by far the vainest girl he'd ever met. But I was determining my fate. I had overheard a conversation between Mum and Dad. They feared that I was not going to be a beauty. And from looking at photographs of the time, I can see that I was certainly not promising as a femme fatale. My eyebrows were high and rounded, my nose was the largest feature on my face, I had a weak chin, I walked with an apologetic hump. I swear it was by force of will that I was able to transform in any measure.

I remember ambling along the gravel driveway after Mum and Dad as they toured the site of the Big House with their architect, Michael Scott. Two medieval stone lions had been installed and were gazing out placidly from beside the columns at the entrance of a three-story Georgian manor composed of pale limestone blocks and tall windows with rounded cornices. My father once said, "The house itself was one of the most beautiful in all Ireland." They were painstakingly restoring its graceful lines and taking out the extra walls that had partitioned the generous and beautifully proportioned formal rooms during the Victorian era. Mum was designing the interior, choosing colors and fabrics to create a background for the many extraordinary and diverse objects in my father's personal collection—Greek marbles, Venetian glass, dancing Indian Shivas, Japanese screens and woodblocks, retablos, Chinese gongs, Italian carvings, bronzes, guns, ancient weaponry, Imperial jade, Etruscan gold, French tapestries, Louis XIV furniture, an eclectic assortment of fine paintings, and an important collection of pre-Columbian and African art from his trips to Mexico and the Congo.

Dad collected people as well. Like his grandfather John Gore, who once appeared home from a trip with a boy, Henry, whom he claimed to have adopted, Dad had adopted a child, Pablo, while making *The Treasure of the Sierra Madre,* in Mexico. We'd met him only once or twice, but we understood that he belonged to Dad's last life, in America. Pablo was a good deal older than Tony and me, married now, and living in California, and no longer seemed to be part of the collection.

Dad's stories usually started with a long, deep pause at the beginning, as if reckoning with the narrative, his head thrown back, his brown eyes searching to visualize the memory, taking time to measure and reflect. There were a lot of "ums" and drawings on his cigar. Then the tale would begin.

He talked about the war. During the shooting of a documentary for the War Department at the Battle of San Pietro, the 143rd Regiment needed eleven hundred new troops to come in after the initial combat. Steel cable was stretched across the Rapido River to allow the troops to cross at night to the other side. But the Germans struck and the soldiers took a terrible hit. On the opposite side of the river, a major stood waist-deep in the water, his hand blasted off, and saluted each of the soldiers as they crossed. Dad said, "I never gave a sloppy salute again."

There was the story of a crash landing in Adak, when Dad was filming another documentary, *Report from the Aleutians.* On his first flight out on a B-24, the plane's brakes had frozen when they came in for a landing, skidding and slicing off the wings of two other B-24s on the runway. When the plane came to a halt, someone shouted to get out fast before it exploded. Dad tried to photograph the rescue team as they came aboard in an attempt to revive the unconscious pilot and copilot, but realized that he was shaking too hard to take the picture. He "put the camera down, and ran." Mercifully, the explosion never happened. Dad told of another flight, over Kiska, an island in the Aleutians, when the Japanese pilots attacked and he tried to photograph the air battle over the body of the waist gunner, who had been killed in action.

He described being in Rome at Thanksgiving, when American trucks poured into town stacked high with plucked turkeys. His terrible revulsion at seeing this spectacle rendered him unable to eat poultry for the rest of his life.

Dad's stories were quite like his movies—triumph and/or disaster in the face of adversity; the themes were manly. The stories often took place in foreign, exotic places with an emphasis on wildlife, which we loved. We begged to hear our favorite ones from the location of *The African Queen*: the marching red ants that ate everything they came across, and how the crew had to dig trenches, fill them with gasoline, and set them on fire because it was the only way to stop the ants from devouring everything in their path. There was the story of the missing villager whose pinkie finger turned up in the stew, and the hunt for the bull elephant and of being downwind of a water buffalo. And the one where the whole crew was suffering from dysentery, which was holding up the shoot, until a deadly poisonous black mamba was discovered wrapped around the latrine. Dad would laugh. "Suddenly, no one had to go to the bathroom anymore!"

For a short while a mannish German, Miss Perry, worked as a housekeeper up at the Big House, and Paddy Coyne came to work for us as a houseboy at the Little House. He had grown up in an orphanage in Cork; he was short and strong, with ebony eyes and a shock of black hair. Kitty was one of the staff that had come to St. Clerans from Courtown. She had a hooked nose and looked like the drawings of Granny in the *Addams Family* book. It took little effort for me to persuade Kitty to remove her dental bridge, shine a flashlight under her chin, and, wrapped in a sheet, chase Tony, me, and the Lynch kids up and down a darkened passage at the back of the Big House as we screamed in terror.

Betts would come down from her home in Kilcullen, and she, Paddy Lynch, and my parents would go on outings to Connemara, Clare, Cork, and Limerick to scout the fields for horses. One such search led to the discovery of Blue Jeans, a horse that competed in the Olympics after Dad sold it. Another was the several-times winner of the Galway Championship Stone Wall, the winning show jumper at the Dublin Horse Show, the main trophy winner at Mountbellew in 1957, and the winner of two trophies later at Ballinasloe Fair. Mum had spotted a magnificent bay gelding on a range of mountains near Clifden called the Twelve Pins, and Dad had bought him for a song. Mum had christened him Errigal.

To John from Ricki
November 8, 1957

My horse Errigal is going like a dream; I had him out yesterday, on the roads and in the field, and his mouth is so light you can do anything with him; this week had been push and go personified; and it has been about five in the evening, on two occasions, when we have ridden out, and yesterday was the first good daylight work he'd had all week. Riding in the evening has been something special and marvelous, though. The weather, since Monday, has been clear and clearer; yesterday was the first hard frost, and again this morning the garden lay somnolent under the glazing. The sky has blazed blue, the remaining few Beech leaves are brazen against the sky; the world is so fragilely, delicately still, it seems it must break. Riding in the bleached blue light of the moon was extraordinary— the air so clear and perfectly cold, temperature ideal for the life of a horse. Last night was the full, the moon rose bright blush pink, the same color as old, well cared for copper, so bright at first that the stars were quite outshone, save for one impudent—probably Venus—who defied extinguishing.

My mother was out of her element in the rough West Country, trying to do everything beautifully. She was an exotic fish out of water, even though she made a good effort. She'd organized a hunt ball early on at St. Clerans. It was the dead of winter. The temperature was subzero. She put up a marquee in the Little House yard—Guinness and champagne were to be served. And oysters brought up from Paddy Burkes pub in Clarinbridge. And a band. She was wearing a white strapless taffeta evening dress. It was twinkling with hoarfrost inside the marquee, so cold that no one could bear to go out that night. I remember my mother, her eyes shining, hovering alone at the entrance as the band packed up their instruments early to go home. She was as beautiful, as translucent and remote, as one of the photographs I'd seen in the ballet books she had given to me, like Pavlova or the Queen of the Willis in *Giselle*.

Over the summer, Tony and I went with Nurse and Mum to Achill Island for a few weeks' holiday. Joined to the mainland by a causeway and fringed with deep-purple heather, Achill is an outcropping of limestone, where much of the amethyst in Ireland is quarried. A small hotel and a couple of shops were the only concessions to the outside world. Along the drive, there were thatched cottages, few and far between. Tony fished and I gathered seashells with Nurse on the beach near the harbor, where the black curraghs came in off the Atlantic with their catches of silver mackerel like lost souls on the end of catgut lines of colored feathers.

Mum and Nora Fitzgerald, a good friend of my parents' and Dublin's premier wine merchant, would occasionally go out into the countryside by night and saw down billboards that they thought were a blight to the landscape. I remember some pranks of theirs, like stealing an enormous iron key and locking the baronial doors to the dining room of a hotel called Ashford Castle, trapping all the guests eating lunch inside. Then off they went, cackling.

Mum and Nora had another big joke between them, "The Merkin Society," and any stray sheep's wool snagged on a line of barbed wire was fertile ground for hilarity. Although I had no idea that the source of this joke was the rather specialized information that a merkin was in fact a pubic wig, I sought to join their evident enjoyment by procuring some animal stickers at Woolworth's and affixing them to the doors of the Little House with handwritten messages that went "Start the day the merkin way!" and "A merkin a day keeps the doctor away!" Evidently I had struck the right note, as this seemed to vastly amuse them.

CHAPTER 5

Tony, Ricki, and Anjelica, Klosters,
Switzerland, March 1959

Designed by the architect Richard Morrison, the Big House had been built in 1784. There was a fountain on the front lawn that Dad had found in Paris, and a ha-ha beyond it—a sunken wall that allowed for an unobstructed view across the wide horse pasture, with its two wind-and-rain-battered oak trees. The turf-brown river ran alongside, with daffodils on its banks, midges skating on the surface, and red-beaked moorhens nesting in the brackish reeds and dogwood at the river's edge, icy cold when Tony and I waded in to fill a jam jar with glossy little eels, our legs so white, we looked phosphorescent in the bog water.

The front door to the Big House was moss green, and on it hung a large brass knocker—a nobleman's hand, with a lace cuff, holding a ball. You would hear it echo inside on the polished black marble floor of the front hall, with its imprint of fossils and ancient shells. To the right was the dining room. The walls were papered in a reproduction of a Kenzo screen, which Dad had a printmaker make up in Japan—a bird standing on a flowering stump of wood. The tiered Italian candelabra was hand-lit at night, and the long mahogany table shone with Georgian silver and Waterford crystal. Across the hall was the drawing room, its colors pale gold, gray, pink, and turquoise. Dad had found a gold-leaf sunburst in a Mexican church, which sprayed across the ceiling, from the center of which hung an eighteenth-century French chandelier. A Tang horse lifted a graceful foreleg. A large, incandescent Monet *Water Lily* hung on the south wall.

The inner hall, with terra-cotta walls and an Aubusson carpet, boasted an extremely well-supplied bar. The study walls were painted Gauloises blue, and curtains of red báinín wool hung by the tall windows. Dad's art books occupied a full wall above a mahogany cabinet that contained a record player and supported three large Veracruz figures sitting cross-legged atop it.

In a spacious kitchen clad in antique tiles shipped from Mexico, there was an oil painting of a barefoot, airborne Madonna, raising her fingers in a blessing. A bow window looked out onto my octagonal playhouse, outfitted with a small cast-iron stove on which I would fry in butter the tiny potato chips that Dad loved. The playhouse once was a dairy to the main house, and the small ruin of a monastery beside it was now largely overgrown. When the house was being restored, some workmen who were connecting a water pipe dug up two human skeletons. The Gardaí were brought down from Dublin, but it was soon determined that the deceased were monks who had met their fate peacefully, in the previous century.

Behind the kitchen were the pantry and the TV room, where we watched the first heavyweight prizefight televised in Ireland—the collision of Cassius Clay and Sonny Liston. Dad wrote in his autobiography, "The little TV room would be thick with smoke and expletives, the staff would join in modestly but with gusto; we were on common ground."

There was a larder in the basement where the kills of the day were hung, mostly birds that had seen the wrong end of Tony's gun—wood pigeon, grouse, duck, snipe. At dinner you had to watch out not to break your teeth on the shot pellets that brought them down.

The Gun Room had French doors that opened out onto a stone-and-concrete moat surrounding the house like a secret passage. On the bright forest-green walls hung taxidermy game that my father had shot in Africa and India—the head of a snarling young tiger hung opposite a placidly bovine water buffalo. The pelt of the tiger lay underfoot next to a pool table lined in red felt. Several impala gazed on the locked-down rifles with the glassy-eyed, dumb expressions of the unfortunately surprised. Next door, the office, with its top shelf of Oscars and other awards, was the destination of the long phone calls, the heated discussions with the business managers.

Down the hall was the wine cellar. My mother had created an area by the back door for flower arranging, and original Toulouse-Lautrec posters from the Moulin Rouge hung on the surrounding walls.

When Dad returned from filming *The Barbarian and the Geisha,* he was enchanted by the ways of the Orient. He installed a full Japanese bath, which cooked at a temperature almost high enough to boil an egg, and imported shoji doors and mats and some large Japanese rocks from Hokkaido, despite the fact that similar stones littered the fields of Co. Galway. When we tried to circumnavigate the nudity rules and chose to wear bathing suits, we were seriously admonished by Dad, whose tolerance for our apparent lack of sophistication in these matters was obviously strained.

On the top floor of the Big House, two carved mermaids from a Mexican church organ decorated the landing. All the upstairs rooms had fireplaces—even the bathrooms. Off the staircase was the Napoleon Room, so called because of its lavish Empire bed. Next door was the Lavender Room, a little claustrophobic, with French cotton fabric depicting shepherdesses lining the walls. And opposite, the Bhutan Room, with persimmon-and-indigo silk-embroidered curtains.

The Red Sitting Room separated the Grey Room from my father's wing on the upper landing. On special occasions, we would meet there by candlelight at sunset for drinks or champagne before dinner. It was an exquisite little room, with an open fireplace and flocked wallpaper the color of old poppies and a pale-blue-and-green Juan Gris harlequin on the wall. In the center of the room was a mysterious *pietra dura* Florentine table from the eighteenth century inlaid with colored stone to create an image of scattered playing cards, a dagger, a key, a ring, and a rose. The Grey Room was the most beautiful guest room in the Big House. Its walls were the shade of a pigeon's wing, and a Renaissance crucifix hung above the bed.

Dad's quarters had dusty forest-green cut velvet on the walls, beige carpeting, and a canopied four-poster Florentine matrimonial bed adorned with artichoke-leaf carvings and turtledoves with necks entwined. One bay window overlooked the river, the other the driveway, the fountain, and the wide pastures beyond. This was Dad's inner sanctum, the hub where ideas were formed, judgments passed, and decisions reached.

It may be that no art object in the Big House was of more unusual provenance than the Monet *Water Lily*. The story went that Mum had gone to Long Island to pick up Tony and me from Nana and Grandpa and bring us back to Deauville. When she returned, Billy Pearson and Dad decided to come down from Paris to join her and check out the racecourse and the local casinos. One day, strolling around the harbor, Dad noticed an art gallery and walked in. After he struck up a conversation with the owner, she invited him to see some pictures from her private collection. "They were all masterpieces," said Dad. But a single work stood out from the rest. It was one of Monet's famous paintings of water lilies at Giverny. When Dad asked her how much it cost, he was astounded to find out it was priced at just ten thousand dollars, an extraordinarily low sum for such a great work, but he could not afford it. He was broke.

Dad asked Mum for eight hundred dollars, the last of the housekeeping money, to go gambling. She told him that if she gave it to him, she was going to come along. So Mum, Dad, and Billy went off to the casino to try their luck. Dad lost all the money immediately on chemin de fer and asked to sign a voucher for more, but the casino would not give him credit. The producer Mike Todd happened to be there and lent Dad a thousand dollars. Dad placed the bet as Billy wandered off to the bar.

A short while later the bartender said to Billy, "It looks like your friend is on a roll." Dad had won his first bet and followed it by another and another. At six wins, the casino was having trouble covering the bet, and because the odds were so low, everyone was now betting against Dad. People were crowded around the table shouting and urging him on. Mum was jumping up and down. Dad was doubling his money again and again. "I was having a helluva time," Dad recalled. And then his luck turned. He lost it all on the next hand. Mum blanched, until the dealer pushed a small stack of chips across the table to Dad, just over ten thousand dollars. It was what the casino had been unable to cover.

"It's okay, honey," said Dad to Mum. "We won the Monet."

There was a brief succession of housekeepers, cooks, maids, and menservants at the Big House, until Madge Creagh, our cook from Courtown House, accepted Dad's offer to come to work at St. Clerans with her husband, Creagh, our charming and impeccable butler for years to come. Creagh was courteous, self-effacing, and correct. In the pantry, where the maids would make little curls of butter and squeeze the oranges for the breakfast trays, he would use a bone on the hunting boots to make them shine like black mirror. Mrs. Creagh was a fantastic cook. She was a round, smiling presence in her white apron, her pink hands dusty with flour. She always had a fresh loaf of bread baked in the huge AGA cooker and delighted my father by learning how to make an excellent Mexican-style chili and beans. The Creaghs occupied a small apartment in the basement with their daughter, Karen, who later would be an All Ireland Champion céilí dancer.

Tony and I were often at a distance from our parents. Although later we would spend more time up at the Big House, for the most part it was reserved for Dad's appearances over the Christ-

mas holidays and the few other visits he might make throughout the year. Then, like a sleeping beauty awakened, the house
would come alive, glowing from the inside, turf fires burning
in every room. The activity in and around the house would go
into a different rhythm; even the dogs had an air of expectancy.
Dad always brought wonderful presents: kimonos and pearls
for Mum, a blue polka-dot Spanish dancing dress for me, a mat-
ador's suit of lights for Tony, a life-size doll called "Little Black
Sambo" that walked when you raised his arms, a glass tea set
from Mexico that Mary Lynch and I put outside in the hollow
of a chestnut tree for the fairies. I lived in the storybooks Mum
gave me, like *Grimm's Fairy Tales,* with its fantastical illustrations by Arthur Rackham, where elves and fairies hid like cha-
meleons among the leaves and flowers, and witches lived in the
roots of hawthorn trees. For a long time I believed in fairies.

My parents were quite formal with each other. Dad called
my mother "Ricki," or "dear," and she responded, "Yes, John."
They both called a lot of other people "darling." I don't remember much touching between them, or many demonstrations of
affection. Once in a while, my father's long arm would drape
loosely over my mother's shoulders, and he might call her
"honey."

Later it became evident to me, through reading their letters,
that my parents had achieved an understanding as early as when
they were at Courtown House. Their somewhat unequal cor-
respondence consisted of long, detailed, descriptive narratives
on her part, mostly typed but sometimes handwritten in haste
to meet Dad's expectations of punctuality, and his terse replies,
generally in telegrams or letters, dictated to Lorrie Sherwood,
answering Mum's queries regarding shipments from Mexico
or Japan. Mum's letters were updates on horses, gardens, the

locals, and us children—she often included our notes and drawings, adding her interpretations of their meaning or significance on the back. Her letters are like affidavits, as if she had made an oath to report dutifully, informing Dad constantly about all undertakings at St. Clerans, from importing cherry bonsai trees from Kyoto at six hundred dollars apiece, as per his request—he joked about the possibility: "The idea is for Lorrie to accompany them, say about a dozen to Ireland by boat, watering can in hand"—to the laying of bets at the Leopardstown races.

In the rare event of a full reply to one of her letters, Dad complimented her on her writing skills and suggested that maybe she could write a screenplay. She answered excitedly, recommending Colette's *The Vagabond* and a book of essays. She suggested that it "could be considered two ways—big, colored and cinema-scoped, with an actress like Audrey Hepburn, or smaller and Jean Renoir-ish, with Micheline Presle, or your friend, forgive the indiscretion." She was undoubtedly referring to Suzanne Flon. She made this suggestion without malice or irony.

When we visited Paris, there was always Suzanne Flon, small with big eyes and a smoky voice that purred like a cat. I remember going to the airport at Orly with Mum and Tony to meet Dad when I was five or six. The doors were open to the customs hall, and Mum said, "Look at him in that suit!" Dad was dressed all in black leather, an African gray parrot with a scarlet head balanced on his shoulder. The next time Tony and I saw the bird, his name was Jaco, and he was riding around on the back of Suzanne's dog, making trills like a telephone ringing. Suzanne also had a daughter of Kitty Cat, our St. Clerans cat. It was quite a menagerie in her pretty little apartment.

Mum went to Spain with Nora Fitzgerald and wrote to Dad from the Castellana Hilton, where it was "holy week in Madrid, with penitents, floats, the Virgin of Macareña, flamenco, cheers, screams, and handclapping along with Gypsies and Roman soldiers from the 16th century." She loved to travel. It seemed that Mum was spending more and more time abroad.

I was six when we went to Klosters, in Switzerland, for our winter holiday. I vaguely remember that Dad came with us and then it was Mum and Nurse and Tony and me. Later Dad considered taking Tony with him to the "heart and gizzard of the dark continent," Chad, Africa, where he would be making *The Roots of Heaven,* but decided against it. Tony was playing with Dinky cars quite obsessively and sleepwalking. He'd stroll into the kitchen of our rented chalet, sound asleep, drink a cup of Ovomaltine that Nurse would prepare for him, and go back to bed. He was diagnosed with scarlet fever.

Around this time, I recall lying on a cot in the corner of the living room, sucking on a metal brace—the kind of thing that you bolt onto the back of furniture—when suddenly I swallowed it. A visit to the doctor, and several days later his suggested remedy of sauerkraut had worked wonders. During a summer visit, Tony and I saved hundreds of frogs from certain suffocation when we dug them out from the dried riverweed on the bottom of a pond that was being drained and put them in a horse trough full of water.

Klosters was full of friends of my parents. I remember a "do not disturb" sign on the door to the movie star Jennifer Jones's room at the grandest hotel in town when we went for lunch, and wondering what she could possibly be doing in there that was such a big secret. The Hollywood literary agent Swifty Lazar stayed there too, and there was talk of how the staff had to lay down sheets on the floors throughout his suite because he was deadly afraid of germs. He skied in a powder-blue parka, with a pair of goggles bigger than his face and a hat with a matching blue pom-pom like an egg cozy on his little bald head.

Peter Viertel was married to the actress Deborah Kerr, our "Mrs. Boogum" from Tobago, and now they were living in Klosters. Peter had been a guest at Courtown House in the early days. He had written a book loosely based on Dad's adventures while making *The African Queen.* Its title was *White Hunter, Black Heart,* and a copy of it was kept on the bookshelf in the downstairs bathroom at St. Clerans. Peter liked to take guns out on the yellow bog near Loughrea with Tony. Peter was very sportive, if a little brazen, in the wilderness. There was the writer Irwin Shaw and his wife, Marian; and the Berensons, with their beautiful, fascinating daughters, Marisa and Berry, who were older than I was by a few years and at the ice-skating rink wore hats with long pom-poms and flesh-colored nylon tights and skirts in matching colors that barely skimmed their bottoms. I was forced to wear the same outfit every day—a cutoff black corduroy dress, wrinkly red wool tights, and a yellow angora hat. I resented this costume, but I loved skating—the speed and grace and freedom of it. Mum had a friend who was giddy and funny, who wore bright cashmere sweaters tied around his neck and matching socks, and who was obviously her confidant—his name was Georgey Hayim. They spent a lot of time chatting in confidential tones and laughing together. I liked him, but I was jealous of their relationship. They often went out at night, which I didn't care for, although Nurse was always with us.

Then there was another man—charismatic, sophisticated, a pipe smoker—called Lucio García del Solar, who was later to become the Argentine ambassador to France. My mother changed when he was around. She laughed more often and went skiing with him and then out to dinner at the Chesa Grischuna. The restaurant made the best club sandwiches in the world, and we children would have marvelous birthday parties there, in which we formed a line and danced in serpentine from room to room.

When we went back to St. Clerans, my mother seemed diminished, paler, more hard-edged. I remember her dressing down one of the maids for not changing the water in the flower arrangement she had made at the Little House, and the girl in floods of tears. Mum's whippet, Pippin, when not out on illicit hunting excursions with the family beagle, Frodo Baggins, would cower by the heater in the kitchen in the Little House, awaiting Mum's return from Paris or London. I sympathized with Pippin. One day a neighbor brought Frodo's and Pippin's collars to give to Mum. The dogs had been found side by side, shot down by a farmer.

When Dad was in residence, Tony and I would go up to his room at the Big House for breakfast. The maids—Josie, with fair hair and cheeks like roses, and Mary Margaret, timid as a field mouse—would carry up the heavy wicker trays from the kitchen, with the spaces on either side for *The Irish Times* and the *New York Herald Tribune,* the expat newspaper. Dad liked to read the *Trib* column written by his friend Art Buchwald. When Josie walked into the room, Dad would declare that seeing her face in the morning was like watching the sun come up. Sitting on the floor, I would top off my customary boiled egg and dip fingers of toasted bread into the deep-orange yolk. The tea was hot and brown in the cup, like sweet bog water. Once, Tony and I had a shooting match out the window with our BB guns, at a Morton's salt box floating in the fountain. Dad supervised. Surprisingly, I won.

Dad would be idly sketching on a drawing pad. "What news?" he would ask. It was generally a good idea to have an anecdote at hand, even though it was often hard to come up with one, given that we were all living in the same compound and had seen him at dinner the night before. If you didn't have an item of interest to report, more likely than not, a lecture would begin.

At some point, he would toss the sketch pad aside and make his way slowly out of bed, casting off his pajamas and standing fully naked before us. We watched, mesmerized. I was fascinated by his body—his wide shoulders, high ribs, and long arms, his potbelly and legs thin as toothpicks. He was extremely well endowed, but I tried not to stare or betray any interest in what I was observing.

Eventually, he would wander into the sanctuary of his bathroom, locking the door behind him, and sometime later would reappear, showered and shaved and smelling of fresh lime. Creagh would come upstairs to help him dress, and the ritual would begin. He had a gleaming mahogany dressing room full of kimonos and cowboy boots and Navajo Indian belts, and robes from India, Morocco, and Afghanistan. Dad would ask my advice on which necktie to wear, take it into consideration, and arrive at his own decision. Then, dressed and ready for the day, he would proceed down to the study.

Every six months we were taken up to Dublin for our polio shots. Tony and I were among the first children in Ireland to receive the vaccination. The train left Athenry at ten in the morning; we would settle into the red leather banquettes and order a full fry-up breakfast from the white-jacketed waiter, who laid the table with linen and cutlery, and poured the black tea into sturdy ceramic cups rattling in their saucers. The trip took about three and a half hours. The green pastures and hedgerows, the flocks of sheep and cows, the horses grazing on the hillsides all passing by to the leisurely rhythm of wheels rolling on the tracks and the smell of sausages, eggs, and bacon.

We often stayed at Luggala, the ravishing home of Oonagh, Lady Oranmore and Browne, one of the "golden Guinness girls." Dad always described the sisters—Oonagh, Aileen, and Maureen—as beautiful witches. Luggala was nestled in a dell called Sally Gap, below a steep, rugged rise in the otherwise gentle Wicklow Mountains. The Coptic windows reflected moody skies above a mahogany lake with a beach of translucent mica that sparkled like jewels when the sun came out. Originally an eighteenth-century hunting lodge, Luggala, after burning to the ground, was re-created as a Gothic Victorian folly. The woods were stocked with pheasants, and flocks of Asian spotted deer moved cautiously through the dappled light, clustering on the marsh grass and heather by the lake's edge.

It was a scene from Avalon. In fact, the director John Boorman filmed much of *Excalibur* there in the eighties. Luggala was the seat of a golden circle of painters, writers, actors, scholars; unlike other grand homes in Ireland, the Guinness household tolerated no snobbery. It was not unusual for a visiting taxi driver to drop off his customer and then stay on for lunch.

Born in 1910, Oonagh was not young, but she had the aspect of a little bird—fragile and eccentric, a tiny figure in white stockings, with the feet of a child. She wore a hairband in her white-blond hair and was often carried down to breakfast in the strong arms of her butler, Patrick Cummins. When we stayed at Luggala, we would have to pass through the bedroom of her eldest son, Garech, to use the bathroom. He was considerably older than I was, and had long hair to his shoulders, so it was a little scary. Oonagh's latest husband was a dress designer, a Cuban called Miguel Ferreras. He too had a son, but the boy was unwell, resting upstairs. He had survived polio. I remember feeling that this was what might happen to you if you didn't get your inoculation. Tony made the mistake of telling the boy that he walked like Charlie Chaplin. I recall that this caused something of a furor with Miguel, and Tony was asked to apologize. I knew that he meant no harm.

Sometimes we stayed at the Shelbourne Hotel on St. Stephen's Green, one of the grandest hotels in Dublin. I loved to eat breakfast facing the park in the yellow dining room with its soft carpets and high ceilings, or to have tea in the long green lounge. Lunch was usually at the Russell or the Hibernian, another gracious Georgian hotel, with a water tank full of angry-looking trout that would show up steamed blue on the plate within minutes. Dublin bay prawns were my favorite. Tony always ordered the vichyssoise, shrimp scampi, and lemon sorbet for dessert.

We'd go with Mum to Louis Wine's antique shop, or to Brown Thomas, a department store on Grafton Street. She was always matching up fabric, or looking at furniture, or paying a visit to Cleo, who made Aran sweaters with a modern twist, or to Donald Davies for woolen, hand-dyed, collarless shirts, but cut long, for women. Somewhere in all of this, the visit to the doctor's office—the cold smell of medicine and camphor and then the inevitable polio shot, with all the accompanying terror of its long silver needle and the dull pain in the cheek of your ass. Then on to Woolworth's for a Carvel ice cream topped with a Cadbury chocolate flake before the train ride home. I can still recall the satisfaction of a pair of plastic high-heeled sandals, flecked with gold—Cinderella shoes, in a brand-new cardboard box with one clear side so I could gaze at them all the way back to St. Clerans.

Dad couldn't bear cowardice. Acts of bravery came high on his register. He expected us to take informed chances. If you had balance and followed the rules of safety, such as learning how to roll with the punches, the chances were that you would survive. Risks were fun: that jolt of fear and then the sudden thrill of having it behind you.

At St. Clerans there was the slide I'd attempted down my pony's neck as she drank at the water trough, which, unsurprisingly, led to my being tossed into a nettle patch. There was a fall off a fast-moving cart while attempting to grab a handful of the low green branches extending overhead; I was swept from the flatbed and shockingly slammed to the earth. I ran into barbed wire and tore my eyelid. Dad bought us a trampoline, and after a backward somersault, I landed with my head between the springs. The horse falls were taken as part of the riding experience and didn't really count, but there was no end to the small nicks and cuts, scratches and bruising of life as a child in the country.

I was on my pony in a field at St. Clerans. Penny was another hand-me-down from Tony, after he got Sixpence. Penny was a mean, gorgeous little Shetland, bright orange with a thick mane and tail. Cantering around the field, we'd go headlong at the jumps, then she'd refuse at the last minute. I would come unstuck and be forced to get back up each time. This, captured on film for a documentary about Dad's relationship with all things Irish, his calling out after each refusal and subsequent fall, "Get back on the horse, honey, you don't want to lose your nerve!" I was smarting from the last refusal, sailing over Penny's ears, landing hard in the turf. But God forbid you'd lose your mettle, especially if an audience was involved.

One day, Tony and I were walking over the Sarsfield bridge outside the back avenue. We heard some whimpering in the rushes and discovered two newborn puppies—one black and white, the other gold with a white collar and chest. We fed them warm milk out of a baby bottle and put them to sleep in the barn. The next morning the little black-and-white female had died; we named the survivor Moses, and except for his weakness for biting people on bicycles, he was the best dog that ever lived.

In Courtown we had a fox terrier named Rosie. I still have a scar on my forehead from falling over her. For my sixth birthday I got the first dog of my own—Mindy, a little black poodle and a fine huntress. She loved chasing rabbits alongside Seamus, Dad's Irish wolfhound, but she never caught any. Seamus was the king of the pack, a noble hound with a wheat-colored coat. Standing on his hind paws, he was over seven feet tall, with a temperament as sweet and gentle as a young deer's. His head was the size of a lapdog. When he laid his cheek down on your knees, you could almost feel him detach from the rest of his body. He had a deep, resonant bark, and his sheer size dictated that he shouldn't be messed with. Seamus lived until he was seventeen years old—practically unheard of, since the wolfhound breed almost went extinct and had to be re-bred. They were often prone to rheumatoid arthritis, but not Seamus. He lived on a diet of fresh minced lamb, garden greens, milk, and soda bread, and Paddy Coyne walked him on the boreens every day. When my father was away, he lived downstairs with the staff. But when Dad was due to return, Seamus would assume his position of dignitary on the upper landing outside Dad's bedroom.

Sad-eyed Flash was Tony's dog, a Llewellin setter of bottomless devotion. She followed him everywhere. Creagh always had a few greyhounds in a run out back of the hay barn. He and Paddy Lynch had a co-interest in a racing endeavor.

Kitty Cat was our first cat at St. Clerans. Dad had found her, tiny and starving, outside his hotel bedroom window on a drainpipe when he was making *Moby Dick* in Fishguard, Wales. Kitty Cat had many kittens—as I recall, sixteen at one time, in the backyard of the Little House, which proved lethal to our budgies: Tony's green, mine blue. There was poor Hortensia, the turtle I attempted to force-feed and then buried alive during her hibernation.

For a short while I had Juliet, a lovely little piglet. Before I left for the holidays in Switzerland, I was hoping to teach her table manners. I returned weeks later to a behemoth. Next thing, she was hanging in the larder, alongside the game birds. To this day, I don't feel complete without the company of animals. The great tragedy is that we generally outlive them.

When Dad's friend Pauline de Rothschild visited St. Clerans, she wore a long braid to her waist and thigh-high purple cordovan boots. Dad adored her. He always said that her home, Château Mouton, in France, was the most glamorous place he had ever been in his life—the way things were done there, a high level of wealth combined with exquisite taste. Dad appreciated many of the uses to which wealth could be put, though you might say that money wasn't very important to him, and certainly he didn't behave like it was something to hold on to, because there were moments in St. Clerans when I understand he was very broke. I heard a story not too long ago that his business manager would be so anxious, he had to go and vomit before he'd have conversations with my father about money, because he always knew it would be some hideous story.

Dad could lose huge sums gambling. Horses. Poker. Blackjack. Roulette. There were times when things could be quite tense in the office downstairs. But although the whispered conversations about Dad's disrespect for money worried me and made me insecure, when he was home at St. Clerans, the standard of living never wavered for a second. There were always lots of guests, the Japanese bath was always steaming, the Limerick ham was always ready to be carved. There wasn't champagne at every meal, but certainly plenty of it appeared in our house. It was sherry and cocktails at seven, then a three-course dinner, and then port for the gentlemen afterward.

I think we were the only people in the county who had central heating, with radiant heat under the marble floor in the hallway. The local dinner guests used to take off their shoes as they came through the front door to warm their feet. They loved it, especially after a long, cold day's fox hunting. "Oh, John!" they'd exclaim. "It's marvelous!"

Dorothy Jeakins was my mother's best friend, even though she lived far away, in Santa Barbara, California. Dorothy was sixteen years older than Mum, but they shared a deep appreciation for things of beauty, and an ardent interest in design, fashion, travel, nature, and history. Dorothy had worked on Broadway and in Hollywood, had received the Academy's first Oscar awarded to a costume designer, for *Joan of Arc*, and later was the costume designer for Dad's film *The Misfits*.

I came downstairs at the Little House one morning to find Mum about to leave for Dublin, dressed in a Chanel suit and sporting Russian Red Army dancer's boots that Dorothy had sent to her from Western Costume, in Los Angeles. I had never seen a woman wearing boots before, other than Wellingtons or riding boots. The ladies of the county wore patent shoes with court heels on trips to the city, or to the races.

Dorothy and Mum loved to talk about clothes and were always sending each other color swatches and camisoles with French lace, pale silk stockings embroidered with butterflies and blue cornflowers, kid gloves with shamrocks at the wrist, tortoiseshell combs and shoe buckles. Packages would often arrive from Dorothy containing treasures from her costume collection. When Dorothy came to St. Clerans, she stayed in the guest room at the Little House.

One night, I awakened to screams from my mother's room. When I ran down the landing to her door, I saw a flash of linen flapping. Mum had left her window open, and several bats had flown in from the garden. Dorothy, six feet tall and barefoot, in a white batiste nightgown, her long black hair flying, was thrashing the air and shouting, "Get out of here, you evil things!" as Mum cowered in bed, covered up to her chin with blankets.

Dorothy's son, Stephen Dane, was one of my prospective husbands, although he was a good ten years older than I. Even at seventeen, he was very tolerant and didn't stoop to ridicule, but photographed me instead, under the gaze of the leering Punchinello in the Little House courtyard, pouting in my veil and tiara. Stephen built Tony and me a very nice tree house in the woods off the front drive. I think he was my first love.

Another dear friend of Mum's was the American painter Morris Graves, who bought a house, Woodtown Manor, in Co.

Cork. Morris was tall and majestic. He made beautiful drawings from nature and had a special affinity for birds; he dedicated a Japanese scroll to Mum, representing her life—a tender stem emerging from the dark earth into an explosion of white and gold.

Mum took me up to Donegal to stay with friends of hers, Derek and Pam Cooper. They lived in a Martello tower—one of the circular, doorless stone forts on the coast that had been built during the nineteenth-century Napoleonic Wars. Pam cooked lobsters for dinner on top of a great AGA stove. They were straight out of the sea and turned bright orange in the pot. They made a high whistling sound when the water boiled, which was startling, but they were delicious to eat. When you drew a bath, the bog water ran brown from the spigot.

Mum's friend Iris Tree had been a raging beauty in her youth and was best friends with Lady Diana Cooper. Lady Diana was the wife of the politician Duff Cooper and a muse of the photographer Cecil Beaton, and was considered the most beautiful society girl of the 1920s. She was also the mother of John Julius Norwich, a man who would feature prominently in Mum's future.

CHAPTER 6

Tony, Anjelica, Joan Buck, and Marina Habe,
the dining room in the Big House, St. Clerans, 1959

The town of Loughrea was seven miles from St. Clerans. Until the mid-fifties, there was a fight in the town square to determine who would be the king of the tinkers. Dad told of having seen two men in fierce combat, one with a board swinging from a nail implanted in his skull. The tinkers were itinerant, but we did not call them gypsies. They were often horse dealers, strikingly beautiful people, with brown skin, red hair, and green eyes. They rode around the countryside in painted canvas-covered wagons pulled by Connemara pony or mule. The women wrapped themselves in thick wool blankets, carrying babies in their arms, and begged for coppers. They spoke in singsong. The children begged, too. By paying out money, you might have hoped that they would leave, but they would come back with double intensity—the lone child or two could turn fast into a swarm.

The main street of Loughrea was a ribbon of shops, varying in size and function, from Sweeney's hardware to Kelly's Newsagent and sweetshop, where you could buy ha'penny sweets and comics. I loved *Bunty* and *Judy,* and Tony loved *Corky* and *Beano.*

When I was seven and Tony was eight, we moved on from tutors to real school. Tony was going to the Christian Brothers out near the lake, and I was going to the Convent of the Sisters of Mercy, on the far end of town, a stern, chiseled edifice set on an incline above the rest. There were several churches in Loughrea, most of them Catholic.

On my first day at the convent, I sang the "Marseillaise" at the morning assembly. The nuns were suitably impressed. With the exception of a few novices, who wore bonnets and skirts that touched below the knee, the sisters wore full habits, white wimples framing their faces, stiff as cardboard. Mother Mary Borgia was my favorite. She was easily distracted. She showed me how to illuminate italic capitals with glue and gold leaf when we were supposed to be having piano lessons. Sister Adrian was pale, harsh, and angular; I saw her drag one of the orphans around the classroom by the hair. The orphans were always getting in trouble and seemed to have problems with learning and discipline. Their voices were hoarse; they wore plaid skirts and blue cardigans and bright ribbons in their hair. Their second name was always Mary, as if they were born for suffering.

I was teacher's pet. I took a pound from Dad's bureau, the

one in his bedroom, which in a previous life had contained papal vestments from the seventeenth century, and bought eight black babies from Biafra. For two shillings and sixpence, you could christen them any name you liked, and keep them fed for a whole year. I named most of my babies Anjelica Mary.

I remember saying, "Daddy, I want to be a nun," and his replying, "First of all, don't call me Daddy, call me Dad." It frustrated me that my parents didn't want to be called Daddy and Mummy. "Mummy" sounded so dependable, bright, and friendly: "Mummy," like "plummy" and "funny," happy on the tip of your tongue. Mum and Dad, by comparison, were plain, lonely sounds; there was no comfort in them.

"So you want to be a nun, honey. Well, tell me, when are you going to start?"

That sort of crashed the idea. I believe that my parents had emphasized to the nuns that we were atheist, so as not to have them attempt to indoctrinate me in the mysteries of the faith, but I immediately took to the religion, even voluntarily putting my hand out for the cane for not knowing my catechism. Simple and effective, the cane sliced through the air and then, in a sharp snap, like the sound of a Christmas cracker, made contact with my knuckles.

I persuaded one of the novices to take me down to the huge ovens in the basement, where they baked the sacrament. She had agreed to allow me to taste an unblessed wafer. I took one and closed my eyes, imagining that I would be penetrated with a vision of God, but she leaned forward and snapped in my face, "Go on! Chew it, now! You bad girl!"

That summer, Dad took Tony to southern Oregon, and they went down the Rogue River together. Tony was learning how to shoot an air rifle, and already he was a good angler. I remember resenting not being included, hearing that this was a father-and-son trip. No girls—that meant my mother and me.

But sometimes Mum took me abroad, just the two of us. When I was seven, we went to the ballet in New York. I was disappointed because the prima ballerina was wearing a plain green dress and not a tutu and tiara. When Mum took me backstage, all the dancers came up and hugged and kissed her. The men wore tights and a lot of makeup. It was the first time I reckoned that Mum had lived a former life. We went out to visit Grandpa on Long Island and danced on the beach together. As I held her hand, she led me in a series of grand jetés, each one higher and more abandoned than the last.

When Mum and I were in Paris, we stayed at her favorite hotel off the beaten path, the Hôtel des St. Perès, on the Left Bank. We went to lunch in a restaurant with white tablecloths and polished glittering surfaces. At a table, wreathed in pipe smoke, sat Lucio García del Solar. Mum was wearing a thin pale yellow wool sweater. Underneath, the embroidery of appliquéd petals on her bra was clearly visible. This had not disturbed me until the moment Lucio said teasingly, "I have x-ray eyes! Your mother is wearing a brassiere with flower petals." And my mother became a little pink. "That's not x-ray, I can see that, too," I said. I was ashamed and embarrassed when she wore something revealing. I was happy my mother was beautiful, but I did not want her to be desired by men other than Dad.

Later, when I was eight, Mum took Tony, Nurse, and me to Greece. On our short stay in Athens, we visited the Acropolis, nothing more to me than a group of gigantic yellow pillars, and took a plane ride to the islands, simmering on the runway in the infernal heat. I am sure Mum met Lucio there, because she left us with Nurse in Corfu after a few days to "go on a boat trip around the islands."

When she returned, she took us to Mykonos, a perfect little village on a hilltop, its whitewashed streets leading down to an aqua sea. There was a beach shack where we ate roast fish and octopus with lemon, and the owner's ancient mother carried the dishes to the water's edge to clean them. Mum said that she must have been very beautiful once because of her fine profile, but to me she was just an old woman in black.

I preferred the gaudy women from the Club Méditerranée in Corfu, who wore bikinis and bartered with colored beads that hung from their necks. Every night, a little girl, younger than I was, danced on the tabletops of a local café for the tourists.

I loved Greece—the white sand and the clear blue Aegean; how bright it was, compared with the soft gray skies of Galway.

Like most children, I spent some time trying to understand the nature of my parents' relationship and the relationships of men and women in general. For instance, I knew that men and women sometimes shared a bedroom, but I had never seen my parents do this, and I had no way of knowing what went on in other households.

There weren't many comparable lives in our neck of the woods—literally, forests and vast fields, under a veil of silvery rain—against which to measure how other children lived or how their parents behaved. My parents were cosmopolitan and sophisticated, but this was the west of Ireland, strictly Catholic and very private. Sex, of course, was never discussed. The matchbox houses off the main road were not ours to explore or to use for measuring how other families lived.

I got a harsh reminder of this one day when Mary Lynch and

I were dropping off some eggs to Mrs. Holland, who lived in a cottage down the road from St. Clerans. Standing in the gloom of her small kitchen, I caught sight of a fine brass bed beyond an open door and politely complimented her on it. Suddenly she picked up a kitchen knife from the table and, wielding it above her head, chased us from the cottage. Whenever we passed her house after that, we ran as fast as we could leg it.

Meanwhile, my own household had its mysteries. Why was Mum spending year after year restoring the Big House for Dad, while she, Tony, Nurse, and I lived in the Little House? Was this simply a pastime she found interesting, or was she trying to restore their relationship as well? Maybe she just wanted to complete the contract, by which time she would have the strength to leave Dad and cast her net into an uncertain future.

One for sorrow
Two for joy
Three for a wedding
Four for a boy
Five for silver
Six for gold
Seven for a story lately told

Whenever we were out in the car, or walking the boreens, we counted our luck in the numbers of magpies we could spot. A black-and-white bird, like a crow in a dress shirt, might descend among the scores of ravens to raid the freshly plowed earth, pecking for worms in the open brown potato fields. Once inside the gates of St. Clerans, there was the contrast of green stillness under a canopy of trees, the plump gray pigeons batting overhead from branch to branch, their soft warbling throughout the day, the cherry-chested robins, the tiny wrens in the bamboo and dogwood by the river, where the heron stood, ready to strike, in the shallows. There were fleeting appearances of a kingfisher the color of lapis lazuli over the waterfall, rabbits bounding under cover of the thickets of box hedge and laurel, nettles and dock leaves—they always grew together; dock leaves are the antidote to a nettle's sting.

In a hidden glade outside the walled garden, I came upon a nest of lily of the valley. In the banks by the fields, there was a profusion of wild strawberries, violets, buttercups, dandelions, thistles, primroses, bluebells, and daisies. Where the cows had fertilized the pastures, Mary and I would go out with baskets to collect mushrooms. In the fall we picked hazelnuts and blackberries. We strung shiny brown horse chestnuts from a knotted string in a game called Conkers, in which you would try to smash your opponent's with your own. Being in the fields and woods was part of the day's routine; there were always places to inspect, to excavate—so many secrets buried at St. Clerans.

I was sitting on the radiator by my bedroom window at the Little House, looking down at Punchinello in the courtyard. The windowsill was littered with dead and dying wasps. "Nineteen fifty-nine is a very good year," I said to myself. For no particular reason, it felt like an epiphany.

We were having our first Christmas at the Big House. Friends of Dad's were coming and they had a daughter, Joan. Her father, Jules Buck, had been Dad's cameraman during the war on his documentaries *Report from the Aleutians* and *The Battle of San Pietro*. Both movies had been commissioned by the War Department as recruitment films, but the message had proved contrary—my father once said, "If I ever make a movie that's pro-war, take me out and shoot me." The Buck family had been living in Paris and London, where Jules was now working as a movie producer.

It was early evening and dark outside when I met Joan and her parents in the main hall of the Big House; they had just come in from Shannon Airport. Her mother was called Joyce. She had short hair and wore high heels and she was very pretty and friendly. She urged Joan to share her comic books with me. I had heard that Joan was three years older than I. We were about the same height, and she looked at me suspiciously. She had a pale complexion, dark shoulder-length hair, full lips. She thought I was tiny and mouselike with big front teeth. Joan claimed to her mother that she had a tummy ache. From her shoulder hung a green leather bag with a gold medallion clasp, which fascinated me. Under her arm she carried a stack of *Archie* and *Little Lulu* comics. She seemed to have a pretty firm grip on them.

I trailed upstairs as the Bucks were shown to the Grey Room. Beyond a gold Japanese screen, night was falling through the bow windows overlooking the wide horse pastures, between the side roads reaching out to Craughwell and Carabane. Joyce Buck pulled aside the brocade curtain that framed the alcove to the toilet in the bathroom and raised her skirt, as I looked solemnly on. Joan attempted to pull the curtain to shield her mother from my obvious interest. Joyce laughed and said, "We're all girls here!" She explained to Joan that she would be going down to the Little House to stay with me in my room. This idea did not seem to please Joan one bit. Tony had moved over to the loft above the stables that Dad had occupied before the Big House was ready.

I don't really remember what it was that forged our friendship, or why Joan, already a sophisticate at eleven, should have tolerated the attentions of a fawning eight-year-old. But Joan and I became best friends that Christmas. I wished I were Catholic so that Jules and Joyce might become my godparents.

Jules Buck was working with Peter O'Toole, who had created a stir in the West End in a play called *The Long, the Short, and the Tall.* Peter had signed to do a film about Lawrence of Arabia with the great British director David Lean. He and his wife, the glamorous Welsh actress Siân Phillips, had been invited to stay over at St. Clerans on their way to their own home in Connemara for Christmas. Peter had blond hair and crystal-blue eyes. He looked like a god. He spoke theatrically, with an Irish inflection. A few days later, Cherokee Hart arrived. At one time a girlfriend of Dad's, she had since married the novelist Hans Habe, from whom she was now separated. She brought her daughter, Marina, a beautiful eight-year-old green-eyed blond, who joined Joan and me, sleeping on a foldout cot in my bedroom at the Little House. Cherokee was staying up at the Big House, and Marina cried for her mother the first night. Marina introduced me to her Barbie dolls. I was mesmerized by them. She wore a red nightdress with a bib that read "don't tease me," which gave you the idea to do just that. Eric Sevareid, the distinguished broadcaster, and his wife, Belén, arrived to complete the guest list.

I only dimly remember my mother's presence in the midst of all of these visitors, but I know that it was from this time that Joan formed her deep attachment to Mum. Joan said later, "I just fell in love with her; she was always ready to play." She told me that when she would see me crawling all over Mum, she was sad not to have that with her own mother. Mum gave her approval, stimulus, ideas, books—opened worlds for her and was the most profound influence in her life. Even before she entered her teens, Joan was an extremely intelligent person with a highly developed critical eye and an even higher level of expectation from her friends.

A few days into her stay, Joan decided that we should perform a theatrical piece for the adults, and, having given it serious thought, had opted for the three witches from *Macbeth,* act four, scene one. We earnestly set about finding our costumes. Marina chose a blue silk nightshirt of my father's, and Joan a maroon kimono. I chose one of the car rugs—a heavy, rustic sheep's-wool blanket. With back-teased hair, I felt the look was most effective. Tony was in charge of the special effects and had been persuaded to click the lights off and on to simulate lightning during the performance.

Clutching our wooden spoons, we took our places in the dark around an African brass cauldron into which an ample jug of tomato juice, doubling as baboon's blood, was to be poured during the performance. The audience—Bucks, O'Tooles, Sevareids, Hustons, and a smattering of kitchen help—were seated in the marble foyer, facing the inner hall. Suddenly, what had begun as a lark turned deadly serious. As I looked out from the shadows at the illuminated faces in the outer hallway, my heart began to race. Tony turned on the lights; there was a murmur and a brief spatter of applause. Joan started her verse and then turned it over to me. Heat rose in my cheeks alongside pure panic. I felt like someone had slapped me. Overwhelmed, I gasped for air. The line "Toad, that under cold stone" rang out thinly and died off into silence. I stood up and dropped my wooden spoon. "This is silly!" I cried, and fled from the scene, trailing my thick black Connemara blanket, to hide in shame behind the curtains in the study. Tony set up a hunting party to find and flay me for ruining everything. The girls sounded furious. Finally, after a good wait, I emerged to seek my mother, to curl up in her lap and cry hot tears into her polo-neck sweater. Not what you'd call a very auspicious beginning.

I saw Peter O'Toole recently, after all these years. He was in Hollywood, putting his hands and feet in concrete at Grauman's Chinese Theatre; he was frail but ever beautiful. After the ceremony, I sat beside him at Musso and Frank's and revived the story of my historic Shakespearean failure. "Don't you remember?" he said. "You caught my eye . . ." And all at once it came back to me—the flash of electric blue, and then the total loss of memory. I was astounded that he remembered the moment.

Despite the traumatic aftereffects associated with my introduction to Shakespeare, I went on to write two set pieces that Christmas. The first was *The Drama of Love,* imaginatively based on the supposed affair between Martin Tierney, our valet in training, and Vera, a slender, pretty girl who worked in the kitchen. The pages were heavily illustrated, with Vera's mouth drawn in the shape of a heart. The other piece was a one-act play involving a pope, a fisherman, and a priest, in which every sentence began with "Bless you, Father" and ended with "Amen."

Other than the botched attempt at *Macbeth,* I can recall only a few early theatrical experiences—one, a vague memory of playing an acolyte to the Virgin Mary in a nativity play that the nuns had put on in Loughrea, and the other, going to see a friend of my parents, Sonia French, from the next county, sing "Oklahoma," which, rather than inspiring me to sing, gave me the idea to create a surrey for Penny, which she of course hated. I hazily recall attending a pantomime with Nurse in Dublin, and a Chinese woman, all done up in a red-and-gold costume, with tiny little feet that she couldn't even walk on. She had to be carried around in a litter, and the bells in her hair made a tinkling sound. Other than that, we sometimes went to the circus, which in rural Ireland usually consisted of a couple of acrobats, a clown, and a dancing dog.

Mum was traveling when I appeared in the nativity play, so I described the experience to her in a letter.

St. Clerans
Craughwell
Co. Galway
1960

Dear Mum,

The show was wonderful, there were lot of senes for exampel, the flower girls witch wore lovely bonnets and dresses, the lourdes where they prayed before the Virgen Mary, the girls had white dresses with vails I was in that and I dident stirr from my place but I think you could hear my heart beat for miles away. Then came the Japanese Princess—and the first play, well, you see there are two plays one at half ten in the night and one at half three in the day. And what I mean to say is that, I was very frighten in the three o'clock and you could see my hands shake and I was so frighend that I frogat my mouvements and to keep my head up and look proud and hauty. But in the night show I did not fuss up and shake my hands and I kept my head well up. Mum I never saw such a big croud of people, dad came, glades came, Bets came, Tony came, Nurse came, Mary came, Idelette came etc. I was in the two plays four times and I loved it I and we got a maveluse clap I forgot to tell you Bye Bye Have a good time in Swesser or Austrer

Love, Anjel xxxxxxxxxxxxx
Xxxxxxxxxxxxxx

The grown-ups dressed for dinner, the women in cocktail attire or evening gowns, the gentlemen in black tie. On big occasions, Dad would wear white tie and a red tailcoat and black velvet slippers with foxes' masks, with ruby eyes embroidered in gold thread. Jules Buck took a series of photographs that first Christmas at the Big House: the women in saris, my mother with her long neck and even gaze perched on a cream-colored sofa among the other ladies in the drawing room.

We sometimes loaded up into several cars and drove out the gates of St. Clerans with the guests in tow, for windy sightseeing expeditions to Co. Clare or up to Clifden in Connemara to see the beautiful clear lakes and have picnics and shop for Aran sweaters. When they commented on the beauty of the landscape, Dad became almost proprietary, smiling proudly. "It's quite something, isn't it?" he'd say modestly, as if Ireland herself belonged to him—his most beautiful and valuable possession.

After these outings, we loved to go to Paddy Burkes pub. The fastest oyster shucker in the world, Johnny, worked there. He'd won first prize at a contest in the U.S. for several years running. And Paddy himself was a favorite of Dad's. They made a big fuss when Dad walked in. The oysters came straight out of the bay. You'd squeeze lemon on them, and they'd wriggle. I thought they were slimy, but Tony used to eat close to two dozen at a shot, then order two dozen more. We were allowed a Babycham when we went there. It was sweet and bubbly, with a little blue deer on the bottle, and actually had a bit of alcohol. I would always ask for smoked salmon and brown soda bread, the best bread ever.

On the way home, in the car, there were songs. I remember resting beside my father, with my head on his breast, listening to him sing, "Oh, my pretty dragoon. My flower that faded too soon. My heart's like the strings on my banjo, all broke from my pretty dragoon." I loved when he sang that song, because the "oon" was really resonant in his chest. And then "Waltzing Matilda," although none of us really knew all the verses. And then there'd be "Alouette, gentille alouette." Roundelay songs, like "Michael Row the Boat Ashore." And from my brother, "Kevin Barry," an Irish revolutionary song about a young man who meets his death by hanging.

In a clear voice, Mum sang the Scottish air "Matty Groves," about a lord who goes away to battle and upon returning to his castle finds that the servant boy is sleeping with his wife:

How do you like my feather bed?
And how do you like my sheets?
And how do you like my fair young bride,
Who lies in your arms asleep?

It's well I like your feather bed,
And it's well I like your sheets!
But it's best I like your
Fair young bride, who lies in my arms asleep!

"Mrs. McGraw" was my forte, another Irish revolutionary song. "Now, Mrs. McGraw, the sergeant said, would you like to make a soldier out of your son Ted?" we'd all caterwaul. There would have been quite a few black velvets, a champagne-and-Guinness combination, consumed at Paddy Burkes, and so the adults would be feeling no pain. We'd be covered up in the back of the car with the woolen blankets we'd laid down for picnics, rough sheep's wool with the smell of oil still in it. There were not to be many repetitions of these happy moments *en famille.* Although it was not mentioned to me at the time, Mum had already decided to leave Ireland.

The summer I turned nine, Mum had arranged a student-exchange program with the assistance of our tutor, Leslie Waddington. A girl my age called Adama Boulanger appeared at St. Clerans. I assume the basic intention on Mum's part was to help me along with my French. Around the same time, a boy called Pierre Edouard arrived to fill in as a companion for Tony. I remember little about Pierre other than that he frustrated Nurse by peeing in his bed nightly. Adama stayed for a few weeks, tasted freedom for the first time in her life, and returned to her parents and France after a great holiday, happy and content, speaking English a lot better than I spoke French.

Mum was very excited because Adama's parents, both doctors, owned a windmill, a *moulin,* in northern France. She found this terribly romantic and arranged for me to stay with them the following summer. She had shown me pictures enthusiastically, but for me the vacation was a torment. Anything you wanted to do, you had to ask first, even if it was to ride a bicycle around their property or take a dip in their pool. Adama had a younger brother, Charles, and a little sister of about five called Angélique.

Each morning we had a tartine for breakfast and were forced to drink a bowl of warm goat's milk, which I found repulsive. Every afternoon we were sent to our bunk beds for what seemed like an eternity to take a nap. Charles had secreted a vast number of cigar labels on the underside of his mattress, and these proved something of a minor distraction during the enforced periods of rest. I loathed staying with the Boulangers, and when

I spoke to Mum on the phone I begged her to visit. Thrillingly, she replied that she would come. I was overjoyed to see her, the only problem being that Angélique never left her lap for the entire first day, which made me terribly jealous. I wanted to sleep with Mum in her bed, but this was not particularly welcomed by her or by the Boulangers.

The next morning, I awoke to howling from the direction of her room. When I ran in, Charles was prostrate on the floor, screaming. Mum's hand was bleeding. As I understood it in the retelling, it seemed that he had come into her room with the intention of playing and, in his overexcitement, had bitten her. She in turn had bitten him back, which seemed only logical to Mum, but obviously not to his parents. After a few heated words between them, Mum came to Adama's room and packed my bag.

I said goodbye to Adama, and Mum and I drove off down the coast toward Mont Saint-Michel, where they made omelets like soufflé in long-handled covered copper frying pans on an open fire. At one three-star restaurant along the way, we had lobster in the shell with garlic and butter, and we drank the local cider. I was Mum's ally and sidekick. It felt great to escape the *moulin.*

The following summer, when Joan Buck returned to St. Clerans, we swam in the Japanese bath, and Tony tried to pull off her bathing suit. Joan told me that she was going to star in a movie in England called *Greyfriars Bobby,* which meant that she couldn't ride horses or climb trees or jump on the trampoline or do anything remotely dangerous. I found this very irritating.

The night before she was to depart for London, I hid her passport in the antique picnic box Dad had brought me back from Japan and denied all knowledge of its disappearance, which convinced her there were ghosts at St. Clerans.

Platinum blond with pale skin, in her late thirties, Gladys Hill, a refined and fair-minded woman from West Virginia, became Dad's assistant in 1960, succeeding Lorrie Sherwood. Billy Pearson christened her "the Iron Maiden." She had been Sam Spiegel's secretary during the filming of *The Stranger* in 1945, when Dad was helping Sam and Orson Welles with the script. Gladys left Sam in 1952 to marry an electrical engineer; she lived with him in Guadalajara and they began collecting pre-Columbian art. In the fall of 1959, after she had divorced her husband and was working for an independent producer in Los Angeles, she wrote to Dad about a project. He sent her a cable: "Since you like to travel and since your job is temporary, why not come to Ireland and work for me forever and ever?"

Gladys moved into the studio next door to Dad's painting loft, above the Lynches' house. We loved going up to Gladys's for parties. She would play Trío Los Panchos or Trío Los Paraguayos on the record player and sing along. It was like a little Mexican fiesta in her loft, with multicolored rugs from Guadalajara overlaying the rush matting on the floor and her fabulous collection of pre-Columbian art and objects on the bookshelves lining the walls. Gladys would pull out a drawer by her bedside, lined in ocher velvet, and show me, piece by piece, her cache of Mayan and Aztec gold mythical beasts—birds, lizards, and frogs.

After a few margaritas, Gladys might be persuaded to sing "Down in the Meadow," which went:

> *In an iddy biddy pool*
> *Fam free liddle fiddies*
> *An da mommy fiddie too!*

I loved when Gladys sang that song. Dad called her "Glades," because I'd misspelled her name in a letter once, and she was Glades from then on.

She was sweet when she was tipsy and slurring her words. As with all the women surrounding Dad, she loved him like no other, but I doubt that she ever had anything to do with him romantically. She was too canny for that. She was also a considerate moral compass who looked after his life: communicated with his friends, made his dates, traveled with him, returned letters, and wrote scripts with him; negotiated with his business managers, his present and ex-wives, his lovers, his gambling partners, his old friends and new acquaintances; and followed him from home to location, with a lifer's dedication. I was always grateful that Gladys was present as a buffer when I visited Dad on film sets. She kept a lid on things, and I loved her for her kindness and decency.

Dad shared her passion for pre-Columbian art, and she became the curator of his prized collection, housed next to the Gun Room at the Big House. Gladys could sniff out a fake a mile away, and it was always bad news if Dad returned home from Mexico from a lone shopping foray for pre-Columbian art. Gladys would sniff, scratch, and spit on the piece in question, and before too long, you'd hear the crash of shattering ceramic against the basement walls.

She had a copious handbag from which she could pull out at a moment's notice practically anything you might imagine, whether it be chocolate or toenail clippers. Though Dad preferred not to notice, the handbag was also a habitual repository for smuggled pre-Columbian gold, and on one occasion that haunted him for a long time, some precious objects got mysteriously secreted in its folds on a departure from Egypt—a crime that in those days was punishable by death. When questioned at customs, Gladys was implacable. Because she was the essence of fairness and virtue, no one might have the temerity to suspect her of any type of moral lassitude; she would have made a supreme spy. However, Gladys was not above releasing a confidential opinion, sometimes regrettable in the cold light of morning, as to why Dad was behaving badly, or spending too much money, or imbibing too much alcohol.

But everyone drank in Ireland, even our local Garda, who came from Loughrea on his bike every year on Christmas Eve to fall, stocious, over the back of the sofa. Drinking was what the adults did, and the abstainers were solemn characters who pointed piously to a white badge with a red cross on their lapels and asked for lemonade or tea instead. It was not uncommon to see a lone figure weaving down a country road at night, or men brawling in a pub. In every town hung the sign "Guinness is good for you!"

It seemed these days that Mum was always away. Tony used to sit behind the bar in the inner hall at the Big House and mix drinks. A little bourbon, some vodka, a drop of crème de menthe, Coca-Cola, gin, Irish whiskey, angostura bitters, with a maraschino cherry floating on top. This he would sip slowly and deliberately before dinner. No one really said anything about it. Betts would pour me a sherry, which I'd favored since falling off the banister at the Little House. And Dad would ask for a martini. He had shown me how to make one to perfection: the crushed ice, the dash of bitters, the cold vodka, the drop of vermouth; how to shake it up and pour it out so the olive floated. As soon as the volume in the martini glass looked shallow, he would hold his long arm out for another. Generally, it was Betty who would perform the duty, leaving the room to refill the glass, but sometimes as I followed her out to the bar, she would mutter, "I'm going to water it down. Your father is one over the eight."

When I went back to the study to present Dad the watered-down martini, it was tantamount to an act of betrayal. He'd take a sip and then fix me with a challenging eye. "Come on, honey, get me a drink," he'd say. "I'm serious."

Dad taught me how to prepare a cigar—how to listen to the wrap of the tobacco and test the smoothness and texture of the skin, how to warm the cigar and pick a hole at the tip without benefit of a cutter, how to light the end from a match and blow on the ember, how to suck in the smoke and then exhale. There was poetry to the art of smoking. If I promised to smoke it all the way through, I could have a Monte Cristo on New Year's Eve.

CHAPTER 7

Anjelica and John, the drawing room
in the Big House, St. Clerans, 1960

Mum and Dad never told Tony and me that they were
separating, so I was confused when Mum started a sort
of slow-motion move to London, in 1960. And I don't really
know whether it was before or after Mum had decided to leave,
whether it was a mutual course of action, or simply Dad's deci-

sion, but Betty O'Kelly was asked to come down west from Co. Kildare to be the estate manager at St. Clerans. Betts accepted the offer and moved into the Bhutan Room up at the Big House. I was still living, for the most part, at the Little House, and Betts encouraged me to move into the Lavender Room at the Big House. With Mum's gradual absence, the place grew more conventional in aspect. Now there were Betts's invitations to hunt balls balanced on the mantelpiece in the study, Betts's photo albums full of fox-hunting pictures and sailing in Galway Bay.

There's a line in James Joyce's "The Dead" that says, "We used to go out walking in the rain, the way they do in the country." And that was what I'd do with Betty. We'd go out on hare hunts with Mindy, Seamus, and the little shih tzu, Shu-Shu, that Dad gave to her.

In her mid-thirties, Betty was an enthusiast; she loved a laugh, was "full of gas." Betts told a story of going to visit an old lady who had lost her son and was living alone in a tenement in London during the war. Betts had sat down to tea and the woman had served Spam with worms in it. When I asked her what she had done, Betts said, "I ate it. It was a luxury she was sharing with me. I had no choice." This was Betty's code of behavior. She was a kind person, and very good to me. She took me to church with her on Sundays and allowed me to follow her around and listen to her stories of being a debutante, and of the handsome young men who had courted her at hunt balls back in Co. Kildare.

Betts taught us a great card game called "Racing Demons." It was basically built along the lines of solitaire but with never any fewer than four screaming, cheating players smacking down cards and calling one another abusive names against the familiar background roll of the dice in leather cups next door in the drawing room, where Dad and Tony were immersed in back-gammon. The first time I ever played gin rummy with Dad, I beat him, which he couldn't get over, and then I beat him again. When we went to the Galway Races, I picked out a horse I liked and placed a bet. "The horse is sweating heavily, honey, it looks tired," said Dad before the race. The horse came in nine lengths in front of the rest of the field.

I could tell that Dad was proud, fascinated, but a bit baffled by me. He knew that I had an ability to channel my instincts. But on the other hand, I was emotional and stubborn and not interested in following his advice. Holidays in Ireland felt strange and empty after my mother left. In her absence, I looked to Betts for warmth and distraction.

In the late summer, the forest rabbits developed myxoma-tosis and flopped blindly across the driveway under the head-lights of our white Opel station wagon. It was almost comical until Betty told me they were dying of a disease that made them sightless. Bulldozers had uprooted the old-growth apple trees to make room for a tennis court. At the Little House, my bed-room had undergone a radical change—the candy-striped four-poster beds had been replaced, and many of my toys had simply disappeared. The underlay of Mum's original colors and fab-rics remained, but it felt as if she were being exorcised from St. Clerans.

Betts was the first person to ever talk to me about our resi-dent ghost, but because she was prone to tell tall tales of banshees and hauntings in Irish houses in general, I took the narrative with a pinch of salt. As the story went, some two hundred years before, a man by the name of Daly was accused of shooting the bailiff at St. Clerans. For an Irishman to shoot a functionary was punishable by death. Daly insisted he was innocent, but the judge, a member of the Burke family, who owned St. Clerans, pronounced him guilty. Daly was sentenced to hang. The gallows were erected a mile away from St. Clerans on a hill. The Burke family watched the execution from two windows of an upstairs bedroom on the south side of the house. As the judge rode down from the gallows, he met an old crone by the side of the road. She pronounced a widow's curse on him—that the grass would not grow where her son was hanged, that no rooks would ever nest at St. Clerans, and that none of the resident Burkes would ever die in their beds. Later, the windows were blocked up for fear that Daly's ghost would enter to haunt the Big House. Naturally, Dad had the windows restored when the Burke bedroom became the Bhutan Room.

Sometimes, on walks, we would go up on the hill to the area where the purported gallows stood, and Betts would point out three spots in the earth where the grass never grew. There was a tunnel, something like an old mine shaft, that you could crawl into, but it had crumbled and was impassable. Betts said the tunnel led all the way back to St. Clerans, but we never had proof of this, and as far as I could see, the rooks nested by the dozens in the old ruin of the tower on the estate. I had heard that there had been sightings of Daly. Once, I fancied I saw him wandering through the study, wearing a green velvet jacket and knee britches.

A year later, without any restrictions in the Little House, Tony was using it as a virtual aviary during holidays. He had met a reclusive expert on birds of prey up in Connemara, called Ronald Stevens, who was teaching him the art of falconry. Tony was now housing several birds in a stone structure behind the garden room. Every few weeks, a crate of hatchling chicks arrived from

Galway, and he would wring their necks, storing the little bodies in a bowl in the freezer and thawing them out as required to
feed his hawks. Once, I saved six chicks and kept them in a cage
in the garden room, but they grew very big and soon I had to put
them out near the stables, where most of them died after being
trampled by the horses. They were big, white, dumb identical-
looking birds, so-called battery-bred chickens—I guess they
weren't meant to live too long in the first place.

The alternative to the practice of buying crates of chicks
was the suspension of a fishing net across the path at the top of
the garden, where it would catch the songbirds as they turned
around in flight. I went out early in the morning to see if there
were any I could save. The sight of those stiff little bodies stuck
in the net, with their feathers ruffled and wet, was nothing short
of heartbreaking.

Tony shot the heron, the big, beautiful bird that used to
perch so confidently under our waterfall, sucking up minnows.
And then, as if giving this wayward act his stamp of approval,
Dad had the heron stuffed at the taxidermist in Dublin. On
another occasion, Tony appeared at lunch dejected because he
had lost a falcon. He had sent it off after a smaller game bird
and it had failed to return. All through the meal, he sobbed. In
the afternoon, he went out into the woods with his gun. He saw
a pigeon flying overhead and took aim. The falcon fell dead at
his feet.

Even with fish, I always hated the transition from life to
death—seeing them hooked with their gills gasping on a riverbank, their scales changing from shining silver to muddy and
flat. I got in a lot of trouble with Tony for tossing his fish back
into the river when his back was turned.

93

On summer nights, Paddy would play the accordion and sing, and Mary and I would step out the two-hand reel we were learning at Peggy Carty's School of Dancing and Deportment in Loughrea. Sometimes on Saturday nights, Breda allowed Mary and me to run a steaming bath in which we bathed the smaller Lynch children. I would scrub them vigorously—Ollie, in particular, whose freckles would not budge, as hard as I tried to erase them from his cheeks.

Breda made butter from scratch in a churn, then molded it into a yellow slab with what looked like wooden hand paddles. Their house smelled of buttermilk and bread baking; there was always a baby in arms. Breda was a woman of infinite patience; the only time I ever saw her outside their house was going to church on Sunday, when the children, still pink from their bath the night before, the boys' hair gleaming with Brylcreem, would load into Paddy's car across the yard and depart for Loughrea.

Christmas at St. Clerans continued to be a grand affair. On our first Christmas Eve without Mum, Tony and I decorated the tree with Betty up at the Big House. It rose, shining with colored lights, from the stairwell of the inner hall to the floor above, the star on top kissing the round crystal globe of the Waterford chandelier. Each year our favorite ornaments would emerge from their beds of tissue paper and make their reappearance like friends you'd half-forgotten. The presents would be piled under the tree. Tony and I were each allowed to open one gift of our choosing on Christmas Eve.

At ten sharp on Christmas morning, we'd hurry up to the Big House for the formal unwrapping of gifts. The assorted guests would make their appearances, and champagne would be served. After all the presents were opened and we were dizzy with excess, Dad would say, "Shall we adjourn to the dining room?" The long mahogany table was set with lead crystal, Irish linen, and Georgian silver, and the candelabra would be lit. Mrs. Creagh would have made a feast—smoked salmon, brown bread, stuffed roast turkey and a Limerick ham, mince pies and bread sauce, cranberry jelly, three different kinds of potatoes, creamed leeks and sweet peas, broccoli and cauliflower and turnips, followed by a flaming plum pudding with brandy butter and port for the gentlemen.

Tommy Holland, a local farmer, was generally the designated Santa. Although one year our houseguest, the writer John Steinbeck, was recruited and proved an admirable choice. He claimed to have swallowed copious amounts of cotton wool whenever he inhaled, but visually, he was perfect. I loved John Steinbeck. He was kind and generous and treated me as an equal. One morning, he took me aside to the drawing room and removed a gold medal on a chain from around his neck and placed it around mine. He explained that it had been given to him years before, when he was a young man visiting Mexico City. It was the image of the Virgin of Guadalupe, and the name of the girl who had given it to him was "Trampoline." John wrote to me often and signed his letters with the stamp of a winged pig, "Pigasus," combining the sacred and profane to great effect.

The holidays were always peppered with Dad's ex-girlfriends and ex-wives. It wasn't long before I realized that my father was making love to many of the women who I thought were my friends at St. Clerans. By now, I had a fair idea of what this meant, Joan and I having witnessed the furious mating of a stallion and mare in the back courtyard below the windows in

Dad's loft, an event that had rendered us wide-eyed and literally speechless. I didn't know when I was little that he'd been married three times before. I only really became aware of that later on, when there was talk of his first wife, who I'd heard became an alcoholic.

And I knew about Evelyn Keyes because there was a story that he told about a monkey he'd owned when they were married and how the monkey had objected to its cage. He'd allowed the monkey to spend the night in the bedroom. When the curtains were drawn in the morning, the room was destroyed. Evelyn's clothes were in shreds, and the monkey had defecated all over her underwear. It was the end of the line for poor Evelyn, who cried, "John, it's the monkey or me!" To which Dad replied, "I'm sorry, honey, I just can't bear to be parted from the monkey." Evelyn came to St. Clerans one Christmas, at a time when she was married to the bandleader Artie Shaw. She appeared to me totally mad. She bounded around in a series of velour jumpsuits. I don't think she ever went outside the house, but she complained constantly about the cold.

There was a girlfriend called Lady Davina with a very upper-class British accent. I used to imitate her, much to Dad's amusement. There was a pretty brunette American conquest called Gayle Garnett, who sent recordings of her love songs. There was Min Hogg, who was young and arty, had long dark hair, and wore black most of the time. Min let me wear her fishnet stockings and high-heeled shoes, so I could practice walking like a fashion model, up and down the driveway. There was the novelist Edna O'Brien. I met Edna one morning on the bridge to the Big House. She was attempting to write a screenplay for Dad. I think it was *The Lonely Passion of Judith Hearne.* She was in tears. "Your father is a terrible man," she said, "a cruel, dangerous man." The patrician beauty Marietta Tree, an American socialite who represented the United States on the United Nations Commission on Human Rights under President Kennedy, was a visitor. Dad remained devoted to her all his life. He was particularly proud showing her around St. Clerans, offering his arm to her to walk in to dinner, her printed chiffon caftan billowing like a butterfly as they crossed the hallway.

And there was Zoë Sallis, who looked like an Indian princess. I remember Zoë in a white angora V-neck sweater, ballet slippers, and black capris. She showed me how to make a ducktail on the outer corners of my eyes with her Max Factor eyeliner. She had beautiful, slanting brown eyes, like Sophia Loren. Tony put a live rooster behind the Japanese screen in the Grey Room when Zoë first came to stay at St. Clerans. I'm not sure what he expected from this exercise, since no one, least of all himself, would be awake to witness the joke, and I would guess that Zoë was sleeping with Dad in his room at the time.

I remember Tony taking me up to Dad's bathroom and opening a small wooden Japanese box inlaid with mother-of-pearl. He pulled out some pictures of a blond, naked to the waist, with a handwritten caption, "Looking forward to seeing you, John." I felt a drumroll in my heart. I wasn't prepared for it. Later I came to recognize her as an actress he was seeing during the making of *Freud* when I went to visit him on that set.

There was Afdera Fonda, Henry Fonda's fourth wife. She wore Hermès scarves and Pucci silk blouses; like Evelyn, she never left the house. Valeria Alberti, an Italian countess. Very cool, a little boyish. She had piercing brown eyes, acne scars, and a good suntan. She looked like she'd been out on a beach all her life. She didn't speak a word of English, but she laughed at everything Dad had to say.

My father's girlfriends were very diverse. Some of them desperately wanted to get up on the horses to impress him; they'd assure Dad that they were great riders. They'd be mounted on the calmest of the rather hefty thoroughbreds in the stable, and invariably there'd be some drama, and it would become blatantly evident that they had no experience whatsoever. Dad would find this vastly amusing. And one couldn't help but agree with him because they were so earnest. "Oh, yes, John, I ride!"

CHAPTER 8

Anjelica riding sidesaddle in the film *Sinful Davey*, 1968

Tulara Castle, on the Shannon Road, was the home of the Hemphills. Their children, Angela and Charles, were our age and we went to each other's birthday parties. Sometimes in the summer, Peter Patrick would take Betts and us out from Galway Bay on his yacht to Bird Island. We would bring a picnic basket from Mrs. Creagh filled with tuna and chicken and sardine and tomato sandwiches, cut in triangles on sliced white bread. We'd feed the crusts to the seagulls as we left the harbor. Even in the summer, the weather was patchy, and often there were huge green-gray swells where the sea opened out.

Peter Patrick was always in good humor and was an excellent sailor. On Bird Island you could see the whole evolution of seals, gulls, and cormorants on a landmass, white with guano, from eggs to fledglings to the adults sitting on the eggs, and the occasional sacrifice—a mass of feathers on the black rocks covered with limpets and dark blue mussels turned brown from iodine and sun. We would clamber ashore for twenty minutes to be a part of the cacophony of bird life, but the scent of fish and bird droppings was intense, and it was hard to watch the desperate efforts these creatures made to exist. The cormorant hatchlings had necks like serpents and shrieked like the devil at the encroaching seals.

The first time we were on the boat, the problem arose of how and when to use the bucket that served as our toilet. It was situated directly under a trapdoor in the hold and was a source of much teasing and amusement. I had no intention of using the thing, God forbid; I would hold everything in until I got home. On the way back, the worst happened, and I couldn't restrain nature's urgent call. I sat in my soiled jeans for the next two hours back to the harbor in the skiff, then a further hour in the car. I kept as silent as the grave. When we drove through the Little House gates, it was dark. I ran upstairs, got out of my filthy jeans, put them in a brown paper bag, ran down to the river, and threw the bag in, below the second waterfall downstream, as far as I could.

It was 1961. Dad was gone for a long time in Reno, Nevada, during production of *The Misfits*. I remember turning the pages in a portfolio of publicity shots for the movie, taken by the photographer Eve Arnold. The actress was white-blond, with an expression that changed from tears to laughter on each page. In some of the pictures, she was backlit, and you could see how her cheeks were dusted with down like a ripe peach. She was beautiful from every angle. Her name was Marilyn Monroe.

When Dad finally came home, he went out hunting on Frisco, fell off going over a stone wall, and broke his leg. He was laid out on a stretcher on the floor of the study; they were taking him to the Carmelite hospital in Galway. Although he was joking, I sensed he was in pain. They had to reset his leg. Dad loved the nuns, and they loved him too, indulging him by allowing him to sneak an Irish whiskey at bedtimes.

Billy Pearson, Dad's sidekick and dedicated companion, came to visit at St. Clerans. He'd get up at the dinner table and gleefully recount his and Dad's wild adventures, the stories becoming increasingly exaggerated. Like the story of the camel race they agreed to compete in on the streets of Virginia City, Nevada. Four riders were involved, but Dad had worked out a plan whereby he was sure he could win, having arranged to have his camel trained by being taken out to the starting line, then returned to the barn and fed, twice a day before the event.

On the day of the race, Billy was dressed in jockey silks and Dad in jodhpurs; they arrived in an antique car after a champagne breakfast in Reno, and everyone in town was three sheets to the wind. Billy's camel started off at an angle, scattering the crowd, jumped onto the bed of a pickup truck, cleared a Thunderbird, and finally, going full tilt, disappeared into Piper's Opera House, with Billy hanging on for dear life. Dad's camel ran swiftly to the barn without incident. After the race, when Dad was interviewed on the radio, he declared, "Billy Pearson is an obvious disgrace to the camel-riding profession. He rode over parked cars, widows, orphans. In fact, there are camel-stunned babies scattered all over these historic hillsides—it is a scene of carnage, owing to Pearson's shocking disregard for life, liberty, and the pursuit of happiness. He just doesn't belong up there on the hump of a camel."

There was the account of their getting shot at in a helicopter exporting pre-Columbian art, the tales of how they loved to smoke and drink and bet on horses. There was the story of a confrontation with a bunch of Mexican soldiers in Rosarita Beach, when a general drew a .45 on Dad, who responded by putting his finger in the gun barrel. Naturally, Dad and the general wound up getting drunk and singing songs together.

On another occasion, during the filming of *The Unforgiven*, Billy Pearson had gone down to the location, in Durango, Mexico, to visit Dad. A new luxury golf club was opening in town and a list of international golfing celebrities had flown in for the event. Billy and Dad conjured up a plan that was extravagant, even by their high standards. They went out and bought all the Ping-Pong balls they could find and inscribed them with horrible messages such as "Go home you Yankee bastards!" And "Fuck you dirty Mexican cabrones!" Then rented a small aircraft, and while play was in progress dropped more than two thousand Ping-Pong balls on the fairway. As they described it, the joke went off brilliantly. In Dad's words, "A triumph. Nobody could locate a golf ball. The tournament was canceled and everyone was outraged, especially Burt Lancaster, who was one of the tournament sponsors and took his golf quite seriously."

And there was the story of Mum and Dad's wedding night in La Paz. And how Billy and Dad had slept in a flophouse, having secured a room for my mother in a local hotel. I suspect gambling was involved.

A legendary hunt across Ireland and the British Isles, the Galway Blazers was renowned for the intrepid attitude of its ranks and for the stamina and beauty of the Irish thoroughbred horses. Tony, a courageous rider who stopped at nothing, having ridden a great hunt and been at the kill, was blooded on his first time out on the field at the age of thirteen—a ritual that involved having one's face painted with the bloody brush of the recently dismembered fox. Having come home and gone for a nap, Tony awakened to find that the blood had dried and come off on his pillow, but after a minor breakdown, he repainted his cheeks with red Magic Marker, which lasted several days, because he refused to wash it off. I was blooded the following year on my first outing on Victoria, a liver chestnut Arab Connemara cross. Sometimes, if a stone wall was too high to clear, she'd jump on top of it and then off, like a rabbit, and her hooves were so light she wouldn't even knock down a stone.

There was a gray gelding that ran away with me on his first outing on the hunting field, sailing over a four-foot iron gate and taking off through a wood, jumping a high double stone wall before coming to a final stop, spread-eagled and trembling on the asphalt of an icy main road. Shivering, I dismounted and began the long cold hike to locate the horsebox. When we got back to St. Clerans, I was so stiff that Betts had to thaw me out in a steaming bathtub.

Dad was avid on the hunting field. The stone walls were high and the hunting was hell-for-leather. Newly arrived from whatever distant location, without even a ride out to exercise, he would mount up on his horse Frisco, and they'd be off and away. Dad was joint-master of the Galway Blazers, and a benefactor of the hunt; on the field he wore a "Pink" coat. It was actually a red jacket, but the original hunt-tailor's name had been Pink, so to call it a Pink jacket was part of the protocol. The Galway Blazers comprised some forty to fifty members, a broad scattering of local riders, Anglo-Irish aristocracy, and children of the hunt members. Every year, the day after Christmas, the meet would be held at St. Clerans.

Margaret and Mary Bodkin, in their blue uniforms with starched organza aprons, served Mrs. Creagh's hunting breakfast on old Sheffield platters—scrambled eggs on toast, fried mushrooms, black sausage, rashers, the ubiquitous Limerick ham. Creagh would fill the hunting flasks and stirrup cups with port and cherry brandy. The air was always crisp, the ground was hard, and the holly, thick with red berries, twinkled with frost on Boxing Day.

The visiting horses snorted and pawed impatiently with their hooves inside the horseboxes before they were unloaded, some whinnying with excitement. Drop-ins from other hunts, or farmers with unshod horses, were out for the sport and nothing was getting in their way. Betts called them the Lions and Tigers, and they were a good reason not to get left behind—they'd ride right over you. This was exemplified for me one day when Victoria's girth broke and I found myself under her, side-saddle, at full gallop. Nobody paused to give me a hand. Dad thought women looked beautiful riding sidesaddle, but it's risky and easy for a riding habit to get tangled, and potentially dangerous if a horse rolls. Though I hadn't really had a formal sidesaddle education, I was a good rider and Dad knew that.

The last vehicle to unload was that of the master of foxhounds, Paddy Pickersgill, transporting the pack from Craughwell. Paddy's two whip-ins would mount up. It was their job to keep the hounds in loose but ready formation, as Paddy rode ahead sounding the horn to gather the pack and we, three or four abreast, paced our horses at a kennel jog toward the chosen bog or covert, pastures bordered by stone walls, streams, and brackish woodland.

As the hunt members were posted around the circumference of an area generally several miles wide, Paddy would flush the hounds through. Followers of the hunt, in cars and vans, parked along the dirt roads, ready to yell if they spotted a fox. This was often not the case, but occasionally a shout would go up if one would break away running flat out for his life, a dash of red against the green, with a white tip on the end of his brush. I always wished he'd get away.

Commander Bill King and Anita Leslie were the parents of our friends Tarka and Leonie. Bill was fine-boned, with keen blue eyes and the straight back of a natural athlete. Awarded seven medals during the war, including both the Distinguished Service Order and the Distinguished Service Cross in 1940, he sank six ships in the Skagerrak Strait, torpedoed a Japanese submarine with eighty-nine lives lost in the Strait of Malacca, and was the only person to command a British submarine on both the first and the last day of the Second World War.

In 1948, one year after his retirement from the navy, he married Anita. She had become an ambulance driver in the French army and had been awarded the Croix de Guerre by Charles de Gaulle. Tall and reed-thin, she spoke in round tones, towering above her husband, with hooded eyes in a heart-shaped face. They bought Oranmore Castle, a fifteenth-century Norman keep close to Galway Bay, in 1946.

Bill King was also an avid yachtsman. He attempted solo circumnavigation on three separate occasions, the first in 1968, when, at the age of fifty-eight, he became the oldest participant in the first organized round-the-world solo yacht race.

On a plywood schooner he had named the *Galway Blazer II,* he capsized in fifty-foot waves off the coast of South Africa but attempted the journey again the following year. Bill triumphed in 1973, when he successfully completed a final effort to sail around the world.

Derek and Pat Le Poer Trench lived at Woodlawn, an enormous, rambling house that looked like Thornfield Hall from *Jane Eyre.* Derek was the secretary of the hunt, an ex-guardsman, and it was he and Pat who had asked Mum down to Galway for the horse races when she had first spotted St. Clerans. Derek's accent was so pronounced, so heightened British upper class, it was sometimes hard to understand. He and Pat often came over to dinner at St. Clerans, and he and Dad would play backgammon before and after dinner. Betts and I would laugh because after a few vodka and tonics, the hair at the back of Derek's head would stand on end, and his accent would become more and more exaggerated, till it was almost a bark.

Pat Trench was always very kind to me and invited me to stay at Woodlawn a few times. Woodlawn was freezing, even in summer. I'd turn to ice between my bath and getting dressed. When I went downstairs for dinner, wearing a full layer of woolen underclothing beneath my evening gown, my hand would shake so that the spoon would tap the inside of my soup bowl. A small two-bar electric heater hummed weakly in the otherwise empty fireplace, and on the second course of dinner, Derek would invariably pronounce the room too hot and move to turn off a rung, leaving one small glowing line of radiance in the otherwise frigid dining room. "A waste of electricity." The sheets were cold and damp when I climbed into bed.

Derek, like so many other Anglo-Irish aristocrats, was having a terrible time making ends meet. Eventually, he and Pat closed up the top two stories of Woodlawn and took to living downstairs in the kitchen and the living room. Soon they were reduced to living in a small loft above the stables, where a few hunters of Derek's remained that he no longer could afford to keep. Ultimately, they had to sell Woodlawn to the Land Commission.

Lord Peter Patrick Hemphill had a soft, kind face and an infectious giggle. A fine equestrian, he was a senior steward at both the Turf Club and the National Hunt Steeplechase Committee. An active joint-master of foxhounds, he rarely missed a day out with the Blazers, mounted on a big bay horse, its flanks steaming in the frosty air. I can see Peter Patrick's red coat sharp in the cold morning sunlight as he lifts a flask of cherry brandy to his lips, then passes it to my father. Once, I watched his wife, Lady Anne, jump her mount high through the window of a castle ruin in pursuit of a fox; a miscalculation could have meant disaster. She loved riding and hunting with a passion. She and Betty were the muscle and brains and the founders of the West Galway chapter of the Pony Club.

The women of the hunting set exuded a thinly veiled ferocity, with their carmine nails and lips, drinking Bloody Marys, their heads thrown back in braying, smoky laughter, a cigarette smoldering between their fingertips. These were the women of the county—the exiled daughters of the British aristocracy, whose forbears had established great holdings and new titles in Ireland in the eighteenth century, under George III, and were fighting hard to hold on. And yet they were more than tolerated in modern Ireland. The Troubles did not extend to the West Country until later, in the seventies.

Betts was a hero of mine. She never looked better than astride Kildare, her beautiful gray mare, her hair curled in a hairnet under her navy-blue velvet cap, just so. Around her throat, a perfectly tied white stock secured with the ruby-eyed gold fox pin that Dad gave her for Christmas, piercing the cotton below the knot.

Sometimes she gave me gingersnaps and cigarettes when we were waiting in the cold coverts on our horses—Gold Flake in the yellow packet, or Players with the sailor framed by a life preserver on the cover. She was an extraordinary rider of grace and gentleness and precision. I loved to follow a few strides behind her in the field, taking on the big walls like a dance.

Oonagh Mary Cusack Smith, whose mother hunted the Bermingham and North Galway Foxhounds, appeared at the meet on a young gelding she had just received for Christmas. One afternoon we were lined up, about to jump a section of stone wall into what we thought was just another field, when the gelding leaped over and disappeared from view. Oonagh Mary surfaced, black with mud, but we could see that the horse was sinking in the muck on the other side. From his position we could tell his back was broken. Someone ran to a farmhouse and got a shotgun to put the animal out of his misery. Oonagh Mary was distraught. Everyone agreed it was an awful thing to happen. The previous year, her mother, Molly, was taken by a confidence trickster called Goodtime Charley, who made love to her, cut the tails off all her foxhounds, and left with the family silver.

In memory, Christabel Ampthill was a person so brilliantly composed as to almost seem a work of fiction. She must have been in her late sixties when I first saw her. A lithe and imposing creature, she had the grace and bearing of a seasoned aristocrat, and until I followed suit, she was the only member of the Galway Blazers to ride sidesaddle. She was immaculately turned out, with a beautifully pinned stock, the gleaming ebony toe of one hunting boot with its shining silver spur peeping from the hem of her blue serge riding habit.

She wore a beaver top hat with full veil over an impeccably coiffed chignon. Two stripes of snow-white hair ran from her temples to the nape of her neck. She spoke imperiously, and most people were afraid of her, me included. But she took a liking to me and sometimes asked me to tea at her fairy-tale Dunguaire Castle, named after the seventh-century King Guaire of Connaught, on the southeastern shore of Galway Bay near Kinvarra, surrounded by wild swans. Lady Ampthill saved many foxhounds from being destroyed after they were too old to hunt, and there were always several mangy, smelly terriers eating scraps off Wedgwood plates at her dining table.

Notable for her part in an infamous court case in England known as "The Sponge Baby," Lady Ampthill had filed a paternity suit against her ex-husband, even though they had been estranged for several years. She had won the case in front of a judge by claiming that when she and Lord Ampthill had guested separately at a country house on the same weekend, they had, in her words, "accidentally used the same sponge."

Everyone was awed by Christabel Ampthill. She was serenely brave and galloped over five-foot double stone walls with the ease of a gazelle. I never saw her falter, but because she was no longer young, the hunt members worried about the inevitable fall. One day, it happened that she did come loose after taking on a ditch; her foot caught in a stirrup, her habit tangled in the hook of the sidesaddle, and she lost her seat. Her long hair was whipping about the hocks of her mount. Betts, through some miraculous feat of her own, managed to intercept seconds before the horse took off over a big stone wall in a jump that undoubtedly would have killed Lady Ampthill. And from her position dangling below the horse's belly, Lady Ampthill exclaimed, "I suppose I should thank you, but what a wonderful way to go!"

There was nothing so close to the feeling of flying as being on a good Irish hunter when the hounds picked up a scent. All the senses engaged in perfect synchronicity and rhythm—your heart and your horse's heart beating as one. Trusting your combined power to fly is an intimate connection.

PART TWO

LONDON

Ricki, Anjelica, Allegra, and Tony, 31 Maida Avenue,
London, 1968

CHAPTER 9

John and Anjelica at the premiere of *Freud,*
Berlin International Film Festival, 1963

I can't remember being formally told that we would be leaving
Ireland to go to school in England, but it was a time of few
explanations. I didn't ask questions, because I was afraid of the
answers. Suddenly, in 1961, Mum, Nurse, Tony, and I were living in a white semi-detached house that my mother was renting
on Addison Road in Kensington, walking distance to the French
Lycée. My Irish tutors and the Sisters of Mercy had not prepared me for the expectations of my new school. I was miserable
there. I found the curriculum impossible at the Lycée. All the

classes were in French, with the exception of English literature and language. I was backward, the stupidest girl in class. I understood maybe a third of what was being said. Math in French brought on panic attacks. I sat in the back row next to Pierre, an unpopular dark-haired boy with restless eyes and a short attention span, who liked to tease me and pull my hair. None of the students spoke to me. On the playground, there was a concrete yard surrounded by chain-link fence and a nurse's station—a little hut with a gas heater, where we were occasionally admitted to warm ourselves in the winter. Tony was going to a crammers for private tutoring to prepare for entrance exams to Westminster School.

Tony and I were familiar with London; we had traveled there over the years. We went to a dentist on Harley Street called Dr. Smith, who wanted me to stop sucking my thumb and told me that if I didn't, my teeth would stick out like a witch's. I had just celebrated my tenth birthday at Claridge's; Gladys gave me a crate of mangoes, my favorite fruit.

At the end of my first year, my report card read *"assez faible."* There's no perfect translation. "Rather weak" doesn't quite convey the French disdain. My teacher, Mme. Ferguson, recommended that I repeat 7ème. I would spend two dismally friendless years at the Lycée, save for the tolerance of Parviz, an Indian girl in my class whose father owned a modest hotel on the Cromwell Road. There were occasional visits from Joan Buck, three years ahead of me in the same school, who dropped in on the junior playground to check out how I was doing. Her interest was the only credibility I earned with the other children.

At Whitsun, the seventh Sunday after Easter, Tony and I returned to Ireland. I picked some white flowers that looked like bluebells and carefully folded them in damp cotton and newspaper for the flight home. All the way from St. Clerans to the Lycée to present to my new 7ème teacher, a pregnant, sour-faced woman who unwrapped the flowers, smelled them with distaste, declared, "*Ça scent des onions!*" and dumped them in the wastebasket. I remember feeling sorry for her unborn baby.

From that moment I contrived to come down with every childhood disease in the book. I was pushed over in the playground and hurt myself. The nurse refused to allow me to go home early. The following morning, when I complained that I was still in pain, Mum took me to see Dr. Apfel, a German doctor with a clubfoot, who said I had fractured several small vertebrae in my neck and put me in plaster from the collarbone to the ears, which was far from comfortable. But I couldn't believe my luck. It kept me out of the Lycée.

Dad was making *Freud* in Munich. He wanted me to join him and Tony, who had traveled to Germany several weeks before. When I arrived, I was met by Gladys and Dad's driver, and taken to a hotel, the Vier Jahreszeiten. When Dad opened the door, I could see a man seated behind him in the murky light. Dad said, "Anjelica, this is Monty Clift." The man was weeping. As I approached, he held his arms wide and said, "Come here, darling, give me a hug."

I was enveloped in a shuddering embrace. He smelled of alcohol. "Go to your room," Dad said to me. "It's late." He indicated a door at the end of the suite. As I lay in bed, I felt compassion and concern for the beautiful bearded stranger.

Monty was having an ongoing struggle with drinking. He was showing up on set with a thermos of grapefruit juice and vodka, and by noon he would be staggering. Dad was angry and frustrated. Although he too liked to imbibe, he particularly disliked displays of sloppy behavior and would not tolerate it on set. To compound the issue, the leading lady, Susannah York, sympathized with Monty in thinking Dad a brute. I had heard from Betty that when Monty came to St. Clerans a few months before, he was discovered in the wee hours attacking the Limerick ham. He and Nan Sunderland had struck up a great friendship and were exchanging loving handwritten letters, which must have contributed to Dad's exasperation.

I never much liked going on Dad's films—his first assistant director, Tommy Shaw, was always shouting at Tony and me to be quiet, and there was nothing going on beyond the set. On *Freud,* the locations were doctors' offices, consultation rooms, and medical institutions, shot mostly in the studio. Dad had engaged the services of several authorities to advise on authenticity and, in some cases, to practice real hypnosis. The English heart surgeon David Stafford Clark was a presence. He and Dad became good friends. Dad's driver, Mike, befriended Tony and took him to the Bierfest, where hundreds of people seemed to stay thunderously drunk for days, wearing national costume (lederhosen and dirndls), drinking from ceramic jugs, eating footlong sausages and kraut, and singing boisterously together. I recognized the blond from the topless pictures in the box in Dad's bathroom when she made an appearance on set as a mental patient.

There was a brief tenure in a flat belonging to Leslie Waddington, at Rosary Gardens, a grim row of Victorian redbrick in Kensington, where one day Tony threw Mindy's beef marrowbone across the room at me, resulting in a black eye. I could see that the direct hit surprised him, but he showed no remorse. I was sad and longed to return to Ireland.

Soon Mum, Tony, Nurse, and I moved to Cheval Place, a mews house on a cobbled street in Knightsbridge, around the corner from the Bucks, on Montpelier Walk. A woman modeled ceramic pigs in a garage a few doors down from our house. Joan and I called her "The Piggy Lady." She allowed us to hang out with her and play with clay.

I loved the Bucks and I was delighted to be living in such proximity to Joan. She and I would walk Mindy and Vladimir, her new black standard poodle, in Hyde Park. He was a big rambunctious puppy, and everyone agreed he was spawn straight from the devil. Joan also had a fast-multiplying family of white mice that she kept in the close quarters of her bedroom. Jules and Joyce invited me to go with them and Joan to see the premiere of Peter O'Toole's *Lawrence of Arabia;* this was my first grand outing since *The Boy and the Bridge,* a command performance for Princess Margaret, which I'd gone to with my father some years before in London. Joan was upset that I was allowed to carry an evening bag, and barely tolerated my presence under the hot lights of the movie theater in Leicester Square. We were to go home early, because her parents were attending the opening-night gala afterward and said we were too young to go along.

When we opened the door at Montpelier Walk, the place was in shambles. Vladimir had committed total mayhem, and there we were—white mice, dog shit, and torn curtains, and us in our party frocks having to clean it all up.

I remember Mum saying that she thought I would like Lizzie Spender, the daughter of the poet Stephen Spender and his wife, Natasha Litvin. A year older than I, strong and tall, Lizzie had skin like peaches and cream, thick corn-yellow hair, blue eyes, and Slavic cheekbones, and she shared my love for horses and dogs. Like me, she had a poodle; hers was called Topsy.

We met one weekend when her parents took Mum and me to Bruern Abbey, the beautiful Oxfordshire estate of Michael Astor. Lizzie and I were in the pantry giving Mindy a clip, and it was taking forever to trim her fur. Upstairs the adults were having a dinner party. Mum and Natasha came to tell us it was time for bed, but we resisted. Lizzie said, "How would you feel going to bed wearing half a mustache?" That was the night Mum met John Julius Norwich.

The next day, Lizzie and I went riding, and I broke my wrist, falling off a young stallion when he tried to climb a barbed-wire fence to get to a mare.

When I was eleven, Mum, Nurse, Tony, and I moved in to Lizzie Spender's house on Loudoun Road in Swiss Cottage for almost a year. Lizzie's parents had gone on an American tour. Tony occupied her brother Matthew's old room, and Nurse was downstairs. Lizzie and I shared her bedroom on the top floor, and Mum was next door. Mum had finally found a house she liked on Maida Avenue in nearby Maida Vale and was in the process of buying it and reconfiguring the interior.

Through Stephen and Natasha, who was a concert pianist, I met the poet W. H. Auden, who took tea in his carpet slippers in their kitchen, and with them visited Henry Moore, whose garden in the countryside was populated with immense abstract bronze nudes. Another friend of theirs was the opera composer Gian Carlo Menotti, from Spoleto, who told me a story about Mum when she was first a starlet in Hollywood. They had met at a party, and because she seemed lonely, he befriended this beautiful girl from out of town, taking her frequently to lunches and dinners. One evening, while driving her home, he made a derogatory remark about Laurence Olivier. Mum asked him to stop the car. When he did, she insisted on getting out and walking the rest of the way to her apartment. She could not bear for her idol to be insulted.

It finally became evident to my mother that the Lycée and I were not a perfect match. I had the measles, and the faculty was threatening to hold me back for a third year in 7ème, when she got the picture. I began attending Town and Country, a school for "artistic" teenagers nestled on a leafy residential street in Swiss Cottage. It had a laid-back atmosphere compared with the Lycée, and was a much smaller school, with the added luxury of having classes conducted in English.

Lizzie, Tony, and I all got the chicken pox. Lizzie taught me the score of *West Side Story,* and together we fell in love with the Beatles. There was one to suit your every mood—John if you wanted smart, Paul for romance, George for spirituality, and Ringo for fun. Sometimes we'd go to Crufts dog show, and the Horse of the Year Show at Wembley Arena, where I would cheer for Ireland's own Tommy Wade on his little piebald horse, Dundrum.

Beginning in 1963, when I was twelve, Joan and Lizzie came to St. Clerans three times a year, every year, over the school holidays. Joan visited for several months in the summer as well. Lizzie remembers being there one summer with no grown-ups around. Betts's father was unwell and she'd gone to Kilcullen. I guess the Creaghs were on hiatus. For a couple of months, a shrewish woman called Sheila served us an unrelenting diet of white soda bread, raspberry jam, and macaroni and cheese. We heard rumors that Dad had gambled away the house. We put on a dog show that attracted the locals for miles around. We made our own ribbons for contests like "Best Fancy Dress" and "Most Intelligent Dog" and served cornflakes in melted chocolate at a concession stand.

The Pony Club met several times over the course of the summer, a motley group of some ten to fifteen children of ages varying between seven and thirteen. We learned the points of the horse, riding etiquette, and games on horseback—such as a version of "bobbing for apples," where you had to grab one in your teeth from a trough of water without the use of your hands, remount your pony, and race to the finish line. We also played musical chairs on horseback. When the music stopped, you had to dismount and run to claim a seat. Tony distinguished himself once by knocking me out of the only remaining chair even though everyone had seen me get there first.

In the summers, Paddy Lynch drove us—Tony, Lizzie, Patsy, Mary, and me—in the horsebox to gymkhanas in towns within a forty-or-so-mile radius of St. Clerans, places with names like Gort, Ballinrobe, Claremorris. Sometimes the Pony Club came together for three-day events. Generally speaking, the ponies that liked to hunt were rarely happy in the formal-show jumping ring, but others enjoyed the attention, and the cross-country eventing was always fun. I loved winning rosettes on Victoria, and Lizzie would be beaming astride Angela Hemphill's horse, the dun Patsy Fagan. Tarka and Leonie King boxed their ponies over from Oranmore, the Lynch children always attended, as well as the Scully boys, and from down the road in Craughwell, Diana Pickersgill, daughter of the master of foxhounds, on a sizable hunter. When not riding, Diana wore a fox's brush pinned to her kilt at all times.

On the road, Paddy would sing at the wheel—Elvis and Jim

Reeves songs. "Put your sweet lips a little closer to the phone," which I always thought was "put your sweet lips a little closer to the foam," with a vision in my mind of a lonely mouth lapping at an imaginary shoreline. Our favorite song was "Oh Wasn't She Charming for Nineteen Years Old," a song about a deceived husband who discovers that the young woman of his dreams is in fact a wretched crone of ninety:

> *She pulled off her left leg and I thought I would faint,*
> *And down from her cheeks there rolled powder and paint.*
> *She pulled out her eyeballs, on the carpet they rolled.*
> *Ah, shur wasn't she charming for nineteen years old!*

We thought this was the best song ever and begged Paddy to sing it over and over. He would pull the car to the side of the road to buy fruit and ice cream, and we would choose from the three flavors in the block—chocolate, vanilla, or strawberry—and they would cut off a slice and put it between two wafers, like a sandwich.

Tony's summer visitors included Tony Veiller's son, Bidie, who first came when his father was writing the screenplay with Dad for *The List of Adrian Messenger,* and Tim, the son of Dad's production designer, Stephen Grimes. We all liked Tim; he was wry and funny, and he provided a nice counterbalance to all that Joan, Lizzie, and I had going on in the way of cattiness toward Tony. Tony and I had found ourselves some allies, and he didn't seem to need to bully me as much anymore. Bidie pinched Joan's bottom under the Sarsfield Bridge. They were forever telling jokes to which I was not privy, so I invented a word, "Witchturla," with which to torture Joan, and told her it had a really filthy meaning.

Often, as the long summer days turned to evening, we

would think of amusing things to do to divert the adults, such as dressing up in white sheets and cantering our ponies up and down the field in front of the Big House as they were eating supper in the dining room. One night, Peter O'Toole jumped out of the ha-ha in his *Lawrence of Arabia* costume to surprise us.

I think it was Bidie who brought the 45 of Chubby Checker's "Let's Twist Again" into our possession. We played it every night on the gramophone in the Lynches' kitchen, and Bidie taught us the Twist; we'd heard it was all the rage in America.

Lizzie and I went along with Mary and Patsy to see Paddy win the silver cup for the Championship Stone Wall event at Mountbellew, on Mum's horse, Errigal. As the judges raised the height of the jump to well over six feet, we yelled with pride when Errigal cleared it with a foot to spare, beat the competition, and won the prize. Paddy said later the jump was twice the size of himself.

Later in London, when I told Mum about this triumph, she said, "If they aren't careful, they'll break that horse's heart!" At once, all the pleasure in his performance dimmed. I had never considered that too much was being demanded of Errigal, and I felt ashamed. When I regaled Mum with stories and anecdotes about Betts and Zoë or Suzanne, she grew stiff at the mention of their names. I recognized the sharp glance, the clenching of the jaw that hardened her features as she went back to being the stubborn victim of Dad's rejection. Ireland and London, like my parents, were pulling away, dividing loyalties, leaving one in a position of constant betrayal of the other side.

There was a measure of challenge to Dad's morning inquisitions: How high had we jumped our ponies? How was our French coming along? How many fish had Tony caught?

"The worst thing," he opined one morning behind a curl of smoke from a brown cigarillo, "is to be a dilettante."

"What's a dilettante, Dad?" I asked in some trepidation. I was unfamiliar with the word. It sounded French.

"It means a dabbler, an amateur, someone who simply skims the surface of life without commitment," he replied.

I hadn't considered the dangers of the condition. From his lips, it sounded like a sin, worse than lying or stealing or cowardice.

Now and again, I sensed intrigue and mystery among the grown-ups, with their raised eyebrows and whispering in the halls of St. Clerans. Magouche Phillips, who had in a previous decade been married to the painter Arshile Gorky, caught kissing Dad's co-producer behind the stone pillars on the front porch. Or Rin Kaga, a samurai warrior whom Dad had encountered on the making of *The Barbarian and the Geisha,* descending from the Napoleon Room in full kimono, with tabis on his feet. He spoke not a word of English but had shed a few joyous tears at breakfast when he was reunited with Dad. Dad explained that a samurai was allowed to cry only a few times in his entire life. For me, who until recently had cried an average of three to four times a day, this was an extraordinary idea to ponder.

Tony and I would climb the mahogany ladder in the study and take down art books from Dad's extensive collection. Volumes ranging from the mysteries of the Greek, Egyptian, and Mayan cultures to his great loves, Rembrandt and Picasso. Dad knew a great deal about sculpture and painting and expected our tastes to reflect his own. The names of the painters he admired reverberated with import—El Greco, Rubens, Velázquez, Caravaggio, Vermeer.

Seated on the green corduroy sofa at the coffee table in front of the turf fire, framed by its veined Connemara marble mantelpiece and Mexican finials, Dad sketched on white notepads in pencil and Magic Marker, his back to the great wealth of achievement on the bookshelves, which inspired and interested him. A high level of accomplishment was like fuel. He'd ask a question to command my attention, scanning me as his hand began to trace my likeness.

I would try not to appear too self-conscious or overly self-critical when I saw the sketch. He spoke about painting as if he'd missed his true calling. I'm sure that he could have been a great painter if he had pursued it as a vocation and committed himself to that discipline. But painting is isolating, and Dad was a social creature; he liked to have people around him, working with him, listening to him, and keeping him company.

Often, when we were up at the Big House for lunch, Dad would beam when Lizzie walked into the dining room. "Isn't Lizzie beautiful!" he would exclaim. And Lizzie would blush. After lunch, Dad might recruit someone to pose for him up at the loft. One holiday he asked Lizzie if he could paint her portrait, but later down at the Little House, I begged her to say no. I did not want Dad to focus any more attention on her. The following morning I took her over to his studio and showed her his paintings. Along with several still lifes and a portrait of Tony with the ubiquitous hawk and his young friend John Morris in deep ocher and brown oils, there was a scattering of pictures of Dad's girlfriends, from Min Hogg to Valeria Alberti, and a playful nude of Betts eating an apple. "I understand," Lizzie said. "I won't do it."

We were all in the study late one summer afternoon. Dad was drawing, the light was dim and fading. Margaret came into the room to lay the turf for the fire, then moved to turn on the lamps. Dad held up his hand as if to stop time. "Hold on, honey, for a few moments," he said. Our features softened as the color deserted the room, and outside the sun set beyond the riverbanks.

In June 1963, *Freud* was screened at the Berlin film festival. I went to the premiere with Dad. Mum had found a sweet Victorian cotton dress for me to wear, with white gloves and a blue satin ribbon for my hair. The editorial cartoonist Bill Mauldin, a friend of Dad's from the war, joined us. They had an easy camaraderie. They had decided to go to East Berlin and to take me with them. A friend of Bill's was living there, someone who had worked for the resistance during the war.

As we drove up to the checkpoint, a little kiosk on the far side of a bridge separated East from West. This was Checkpoint Charlie. We saw plaques and bouquets of flowers and handwritten notes commemorating the dead. Russian soldiers were goose-stepping on the eastern side, which would have been funny were they not so deadly serious. I was troubled by it, but I felt safe with my father and Bill. Some officials took our passports and disappeared for what seemed like a long time, then returned them to us, stamped some papers, and issued visas for the day. As soon as we crossed the border, the lights and commerce of the West were cast off like a party dress, revealing the gray bones of the East. Platforms stood high along the length of the wall; our driver said they had been put up so that people could stand on them and wave to their loved ones across the border. It seemed even worse, somehow, that this terrible compromise had been reached. Maybe we saw a woman with a dark babushka on her head, riding a bicycle, but otherwise no activity at all.

We drove the length of the wall, stopping a few times to climb the lookout posts to see low lines of barbed wire stretching to the other side. It felt barbaric. We went to Bill's friend's bar for lunch. It was a short drive to the inner city, all gray streets with no people. When the friend saw Bill, he wept. They held each other for a long time, and then the friend sat down with us and smoked a cigarette as Bill and Dad drank schnapps.

Dad wanted to go to a museum to see the head of Nefertiti. Except for a few guards, we seemed to be all alone in the place, so dank and gloomy, until we came upon this rarest and most delicate artifact—the most beautiful and legendary of all women, a perfect little bust, smaller than life-size, glowing in that tomb in East Berlin. It was like a little hint of hope.

I was excited because Lizzie and Joan were coming to St. Clerans in July. Some days later, the two of them were giggling in the guest room that Joan was occupying down the hall; they seemed to prefer each other's company to mine. Suddenly, I felt something sharp in my nose, a jab like broken glass. I jumped off my bed and ran into the bathroom. As I watched in the mirror, a feeble wasp backed out of my nostril and buzzed off lazily around the sink. I was starting to panic. I called out that I had been stung up the nose. I was having trouble breathing. The girls shrugged—no one quite believed me. Mum wasn't there, which compounded my feelings of self-pity. I sobbed loudly. Finally, to appease me, Betts summoned the doctor from Loughrea. A half hour of hysteria later and they were all looking on with doubtful expressions as Dr. O'Dwyer peered up my nose with a flashlight. He wielded tweezers and pulled out a stinger, saying, "Jaysus, she's right!" Everyone gasped.

Later that holiday, Mum came to St. Clerans to reclaim some

objects and furniture. Lizzie had just been staying with her parents at Glenveagh Castle, in Co. Donegal, the home of Henry McIlhenny, and the guests had dressed up as the four seasons at dinner one evening. She suggested we do this at St. Clerans. I remember our coming together in the upstairs Red Sitting Room. The girls in costume: Lizzie was Spring, in pale chiffon and jade beads, and I was Summer, in a blue bathing suit with sweet peas from the garden sewn all over it and a crown of overblown roses. Joan, in her favorite brown kimono and a hat of berries and thorns, was Autumn. And in layers of white and gray tulle, with painted red dots at the corner of her eyes, the tip of her nose a delicate blue, Mum was playing Winter.

Dad was making *The List of Adrian Messenger* at Bray, on the outskirts of Dublin. He had decided to become an Irish citizen. Tony and I had followed suit, but because I was under thirteen, I did not have to renounce my American citizenship. This decision on my father's part may also have saved Tony from being drafted for the Vietnam War, which was already voraciously consuming the youth of America. Dad had decided to cast Tony as the son of Dana Wynter in the movie, a part that required a child who could ride.

During this time, my father had laid down, along with the director John Boorman, the outline for an Irish Film Board. Dad's idea and intention was to work in Ireland as much as possible, drawing outside talent with the lure of tax breaks for artists. From this moment, many of Dad's films, through *The Kremlin Letter* and *Casino Royale,* always included some scenes to be shot in Ireland.

Lizzie and I were staying at a boardinghouse on the outskirts of Rathfarnham, learning to be proficient horsewomen nearby at Colonel Dudgeon's riding establishment. Only on special occasions did we see the colonel. He was delicate and kind, a great rider with the straight spine of an officer. We would watch his protégée, Penny Morton, a beautiful blond Olympic equestrienne who happened to be stone deaf, sidesaddle on her bay stallion, kicking up the turf as he flew into an extended trot, practicing their dressage in the vast indoor arena.

Mum visited and decided to take riding lessons. I remember an instructor called Major McNamara, brutal, Scottish, straight out of the Queen's Army, screaming at her, "You look like a bag of balloons. Straighten up!" And my poor mother, jogging around, with the cap on the back of her head, red in the face.

Lizzie and I went up to Powerscourt House to see Dad and Tony on set. Tony was perched high on an outrageously good-looking gray horse—its name in the movie was Avatar. He was wearing the black velvet cap and red coat of a whip-in, a full white stock and gold fox pin, white breeches, and high black boots with a tan leather turnover and spurs. He carried a loose hunting crop, which he dangled and snapped around my head a few times.

After *The List of Adrian Messenger,* Dad was offered the part of the mentor to the conflicted priest, Tom Tryon, in *The Cardinal.* He proclaimed it was all for a lark, but I think he got a good paycheck, and he certainly enjoyed the costumes. Again, Dad disappeared for many months to make *Night of the Iguana* in Mexico with Richard Burton, Ava Gardner, Deborah Kerr, and a young ingénue called Sue Lyon. Liz Taylor was out there too, with Burton, in a village the crew had carved out of the jungle—a place close to the sleepy fishing village of Puerto Vallarta, called Mismaloya.

A story was published that Dad had thrown a big party welcoming the actors to the set and had presented a gold-plated derringer to each of them with five bullets apiece to be used on one another should the going get fierce. From all accounts, there were the usual attractions to making a John Huston film—attractive people, a jungle location, storms, guns, wild animals, insects, and a good deal of tequila. Mum remarked that Dad never looked well when he returned from Mexico.

CHAPTER 10

Anjelica with Allegra in the garden
at Maida Avenue, 1965

Away from Ireland, from the green fields and the open air, 31 Maida Avenue, a graceful cream-colored Georgian town house on a quiet street in Little Venice, became the center of our new way of life in London. It looked onto the Regents Canal, an estuary that flows from the East End to the heart of nearby Paddington. Houseboats were moored on either side, and in summer the light filtered through the leaves of the plane trees lining the pavement above its banks.

There were steps leading up to the front door, which Mum had chosen to paint a muddy green to reflect the water. The house, like all of Mum's creations, was beautiful. There was a large basement kitchen with flagstone floors and unvarnished pine cabinets that looked out onto an overgrown garden, at the far end of which was a wrought-iron four-poster bed, where we lounged after long Sunday lunches, when friends would come to eat or stop by after other dates, for drinks and dancing.

The living room at Maida Avenue was painted, in Mum's words, "Irish-sky gray." She had applied the color with rags, so the effect was uneven and cloudy. The wall that separated the living and dining room on the first floor had been removed, and the light came streaming through tall windows on both sides. Against the far wall, between the windows, the philosopher Rousseau's daybed, framed by the curving necks of two red swans with golden beaks, had made the passage from Ireland alongside the figure of a bronze Shiva. Anemones in apothecary vials were clustered on top of a piano. A Regency chaise stood on clawed feet.

Mum's bedroom was next to mine, off the upper landing, overlooking the canal. She had hung a turquoise Navajo chieftain's necklace that Dad had given her after *The Misfits* on a wall the color of blackberry fool, a British dessert, above an Egyptian revival bed. Her bathroom was lined in antique mirror she'd found at junk stores and had recut, and she had commissioned Maro, the daughter of Arshile Gorky and Magouche Phillips, to paint an angel on her bathtub. Maro was going out with Lizzie's brother, Matthew.

My room had pale salmon walls and carpet the color of burnt orange, with a huge oval mirror, gold and garlanded, with candelabra on either side. Mum and I found it together, antiquing in

Burford, on a trip to Oxfordshire. A dressmaker's cabinet stood opposite, its shelves and drawers crammed with my antique bead-and-ribbon collection, my treasures from the Portobello Road and Antiquarius, and the ever popular hand-me-downs from Joan and Lizzie, who was kindly providing me use of her brassieres, as Mum said I didn't need them yet. My bed was by the window overlooking the garden, with a Chinese flag we had converted into a bedspread—tongues of flame embroidered on a midnight-blue silk background. My bathroom had a fireplace. I used to lock the door, draw the bath, light the fire, and read Marjorie Proops's Problem Page in *Woman* magazine.

Mum called me her "Sweetie Patootie." I called her "Mug." I loved our alliance, our sweet conspiracy. Dabbing on her perfume and sinking my finger into the glass pot with the foamy white cream called Crème de Bonne Femme; watching her stroke dark blue mascara onto her eyelashes with a little brush and making a moue when she painted her mouth with lipstick. I watched her get ready in the evenings, her reflection in the mirror, surrounded by lightbulbs, witnessing the transition from all that I knew and recognized to something that took my breath away. She had bought a dress from Madame Grès for the season. It was mauve taffeta, strapless, like a column. She wore it with the turquoise necklace. The effect was astonishing. I would forget that the eventuality was that she would leave to go out. I understood that Mum had an enormous capacity for love and was conscious of her responsibility to the many people in her life who looked to her for guidance. I was envious, not of them exactly, but of the amount of attention she paid them. She had seen my eyes open for the first time; she was the witness to my first breath. I knew she loved me most of all, and I wanted to come before anyone else.

Tony and Nurse lived on the top story. Tony was keeping his hawks, several at a time, in a little shed in the garden, and was continuing his practice of leaving a path of bloody entrails in his wake. From small yellow beaks to gizzards and claws, there was always evidence of fresh kill about the house. Mum and I complained to him about this, to no avail. He supplemented the raptors' diets with pigeons he had bagged in Trafalgar Square and brought home on the tube.

Tony's room was off limits, but I usually found a way to get hold of the triangular glass Hennessey bottle in which he stored a wealth of sixpences. It was quite easy to lift a few and shake the bottle to plump up the remaining coins. In Nurse's wardrobe, on the shelf above the green high heels with the pointy toes I liked to try on, was usually a carton of Player's or Benson & Hedges cigarettes stowed away, from which I'd help myself to a pack.

When we were first in London, Mum's closest girlfriends were Joyce Buck and Siân Phillips. They were, as Joan later described them, the three graces of the moment, and together they went antique hunting and out to lunches and parties. The crowd was literary and artistic and theatrical. And Joan and my mother had a special friendship all their own, one that made me jealous on both sides. It was possibly one of my reasons for stealing small but significant objects from both of them.

Mum's friendship with Giorgy Hayim was still active, but we saw less of him and more of her new friend and sidekick, a young writer called Peter Menegas. Peter was gay, short, and lithe, with a large head and a shock of brown hair. He had a big laugh and loved a social occasion. They had met through a friend of Morris Graves, called Richard Svara. Soon Peter and Mum were hanging out on a daily basis. He rented an apartment nearby and came over in the mornings for coffee. They were writing a musical based on the story of Gertrude Stein and Alice B. Toklas, called *A Girlfriend Is a Girlfriend Is a Girlfriend.* New, interesting people were coming to the house on Sundays. On warm summer nights, there was wine and candlelight and music.

But Mum was often away on trips, and I missed her when she was gone. I suspected that she was not traveling alone, and my suspicions were confirmed when I saw a group of snapshots of her looking tanned and relaxed for the camera at the Winter Palace hotel in Luxor, Egypt.

I had a girlfriend called Michelle at Town and Country. She wore black pencil on the rims of her eyes and knew more about most things than I did. Tony was now at Westminster School in the city as a weekly boarder, Monday to Friday. He did not appear to be making many new friends in London, but he still saw Tim Grimes, with whom he shared an interest in antiques and firearms. He was taking fencing lessons from a Bulgarian ex-champion called George Ganchev, who was going out with Mum's great friend Gina Medcalf.

I, on the other hand, had plenty of cronies now. Fewer might have served me better, as I was at most times distracted from my lessons and my homework, although I had a morbid streak and liked to write essays. One such effort was entitled "Paris from the Eyes of Death: A Suicide's Last Look at the City He Loves." I was tall, already flirtatious, and precocious; I looked several years older than my age. I loved to dance and I wore a lot of makeup. Every morning before school, I'd draw eyeliner twice across each eyelid, once close to the lashes, once in the hollow, and blend pearlized shadow to my cheekbones. I liked to wash my hair every day, and dried it by flipping it over my face in front of a space heater set to high. It took me at least an hour and a half to get ready, making me chronically late for school.

There was an eccentric roster of kids at Town and Country—Anne Rothenstein, who later married the director Stephen Frears; her brother, Julian, with whom I had a good exchange in Victorian Pears soap labels, which we both collected; and Jan Markham, who became an actress. It was there that I really fell in love for the first time: Joshua Thomas was a great dancer and drew beautifully, including an epic pen-and-ink rendering of Napoleon's retreat from Russia on the walls of the assembly room. He had white-blond hair and navy-blue eyes and a fierce contempt for the bourgeoisie. Although I think he loved Jan more than he did me, when we went to the country one weekend on a school outing, Joshua kissed me between marshmallows by the light of a bonfire.

The first musical I ever saw in London was *My Fair Lady,* at the Haymarket, with Nurse. It was far from the pantomimes I'd seen as a little girl back in Ireland. Before the show started, some people behind us were told they had tickets for the wrong night. I remember feeling bad for them. And then the curtain went up on such a lovely spectacle—Rex Harrison and Julie Andrews. I wanted to dance all night when I got home.

What I loved most was to go with Mum to the theater. It is as much through her as through my father that I received the best acting education, watching the art of live performance. She took me to see Lynn Redgrave and Maggie Smith in *Much Ado About Nothing* and Ralph Richardson and John Gielgud in *The School for Scandal,* with the great Margaret Rutherford; Robert Stevens in *The Royal Hunt of the Sun;* Vanessa Redgrave in *The Seagull;* David Warner in *Hamlet.* I saw Alvin Ailey and Merce Cunningham, the Red Army Chorus and Dance Ensemble from Georgia, the Harlem Globetrotters, Danny La Rue, Marcel Marceau, *Hair,* and even one of the last performances of Marlene Dietrich, who sang "Where Have All the Flowers Gone," appearing onstage as if poured into a sequined mold, in a pool of white light that glanced off her cheekbones and fell at her feet.

Mum took me to see Rudolf Nureyev in *Marguerite and Armand,* in which, from the blackness of the wings, he appeared midair in a suspended leap, throwing off his cape to land at Margot Fonteyn's feet. She took me to see Maria Callas singing *Tosca* at Covent Garden on opening night, Laurence Olivier as Othello, Alec Guinness and Simone Signoret in *Macbeth,* Micheál Mac Liammóir in *The Importance of Being Oscar* (a one-man show about Oscar Wilde), Ian Holm in *Richard III* at the National, and Madeleine Renaud in *Oh les beaux jours.*

She took me to a club called the Revolution, where I saw a phenomenon called Tina Turner. And we were together in the living room in Maida Avenue when we heard Bob Dylan for the first time. Dylan had a beautiful woman, the folksinger Joan Baez. We listened to the Dylan album from start to finish and then played it all over again. Mum also had a big affection for Ruth Etting, a torch singer from the twenties, who sang "Ten Cents a Dance."

Every few months a heavy cardboard box full of the latest releases would arrive in the mail, courtesy of Goddard Lieberson, a friend of Mum's who was the president of Columbia Records. The first time this happened, we were confronted with a selection of about ten albums, including Dylan's *The Times They Are A-Changin',* Tim Hardin, Big Brother and the Holding Company featuring the fledgling Janis Joplin as their lead singer, and Barbra Streisand's *People,* with a photograph of her facing away on a beach in white toreador pants and a red-striped shirt. Mum had a beautiful new sound system, buff stainless steel; I think it was Swedish or Danish or maybe German. It had a little weight that balanced on the end of the playing arm. When you set the stylus down, it floated gently on the surface of the record.

On his way to Rome to film *The Bible,* Dad stopped off in London and came over to the house. He told Tony and me that he would be having a meeting with Maria Callas, whom he was interviewing for the part of Sarah, and asked if we had any advice.

"Don't get drunk," said Tony.

"Don't sing," said I.

Later, when they met, Dad recounted our observations to Ms. Callas. "Do you sing?" she asked Dad.

"Only when I'm drunk," he replied.

Filming *The Bible* was without doubt an immense task for a director. Dad worked on it for close to three years. I received a letter about it from him, memorable in that it was one of the very few he ever wrote to me. It was in pencil and he had drawn illustrations of himself in character as Noah, bringing animals into the ark, a pair of giraffes observing the scene. It seemed as if the letter were written by someone other than the stern patriarch who cast a cold eye on Tony and me during our school holidays.

Darling daughter: I'm delighted at your wonderful school report. You must be very set up. All but math . . . I'm inclined to think simple arithmetic will pretty well serve you through life. But then you might become an architect, so you'd better stay with it, I guess.

I do wish you were here right now to become acquainted with all the animals. I really know them now and they me: elephants, bears, giraffe, ostriches, pelicans, ravens. In a way I hate to see this part of the picture come to an end—and have them go out of my life, back to their circuses and zoos. . . .

Spring has come on, all at once. The Italian campo is strewn with fields of margaritas and the almond trees are flowering. The white blossoms always seem to come first. We've had a solid week of sunshine, the pouring golden kind that you can feel through your coat. But of course now we want rainy dark skies. I mean the picture does herald the flood. No, you can't win them all. In Egypt where we went to get brassy skies it rained for the first time in January in 38 years. Do you remember—I'd hoped to be finished shooting by last December—and I won't be home for Easter. Meanwhile though I have my animals—if not my kids.

I like your drawings of arms, by the way, and ballet legs. Do tell me what's made such a hit with you about your new art teacher, herself, her own drawing, her remarks on the foot that she recognizes your talent?

Betts has a very fine mount for you—or did she already at Christmastime? You've probably heard Sheila-Ann, the first of the two brood-mares, threw a fine filly foal. Shall we keep her and race her or sell her as a yearling and make a quick profit?

The ark sequences should be finished in about a fortnight. After that I'll have about a month of polishing up to do—so I'll have been more than a year at actually shooting—a long time. My beard is now down to—well not quite to my navel, but almost.

Give Joan and Lizzie my love—some of it—but keep a bigger helping for yourself.

> *As ever,*
> *Daddy*

Over school holiday, I went to Rome to visit Dad. He took me to Dino De Laurentiis's Dinocittà Studios, where an entire lot had been transformed to simulate the Garden of Eden, with fake oranges and mysterious plastic fruits hanging from the trees. A small stream of water trickled through a trench lined with transparent PVC. Grips and technicians ran in all directions, babbling in Italian and smoking cigarettes while Dad introduced me to the young woman playing Eve. She was very pretty but not what I expected, which would have been someone more ethnic, someone along the lines of Sophia Loren. Eve's real name was Ulla Bergryd; she had freckles and fair skin and was wearing a strawberry-red wig down to her waist, which I immediately coveted, with a white bathrobe and slippers. I thought it brave of her to volunteer to be naked in the film. I actually received the wig at Christmas later that year, but everyone agreed it didn't suit me at all.

A group of men followed Dad through the Garden of Eden, receiving his instructions. Occasionally one of them would ask a question and write the answer down in a notebook; others would field his questions and offer explanations. We entered a concrete building and went to the makeup department to see the progress on what was to be a full bodysuit for the serpent. They had begun to paint the latex that morning, and even to my untrained eye, it looked a little lurid. Dad took one glance at the costume and became enraged. I'd seen that happen once before, when an antique dealer had chosen to gold-leaf an ancient mirror after its purchase and before delivery, only meaning the best. Now, as then, steam was coming out of Dad's ears.

"You've ruined the costume!" he declared in disgust. One

of the men was ashen and seemed about to cry. Dad could be ruthless around incompetence or lapses of taste.

Dad had recently heard through Mum by way of Betty that I had developed a corn on my toe. He hit the roof. He didn't realize that I was wearing the same shoes, the same skirt, every day. Mum was not receiving the check from the business managers with any regularity, and there had been no shopping outings of late. The next day Gladys spirited me down the Via Condotti and bought me seven pairs of shoes, with high or stacked heels, according to my wishes. They signified adulthood.

From Rome I went to the Taormina Film Festival with Dad. We sailed for several hours on a large pleasure boat with the producers Darryl Zanuck, Roberto Haggiag, and Dino De Laurentiis. Italy's most famous pop star was entertaining the guests on deck, and Zanuck persuaded him to sing "Strangers in the Night" over and over, knowing that Dad loathed the song. Dad just sat there, all the way, smiling cheerfully back at the pop star and calling Zanuck a son of a bitch under his breath.

Just when things were going relatively well at Town and Country, Mum moved me to Holland Park Comprehensive, in the comparative wilderness of Notting Hill Gate. She never explained why, although it is possible she made her decision based on my report card, which usually described me as lethargic and vague. The neighborhood was sketchy, bordered by tenement housing and cheap one-bedroom rental flats close to the open-air market on the Portobello Road. Likewise, the school was an uneasy conflation of socially and economically diverse students. It was run along the lines of a university; between classes, you walked around the building with your books. Having toured the campus, Mum felt that this angle would appeal

141

to me and would encourage me to act responsibly. It had the opposite effect.

At Holland Park Comprehensive, I was the tallest girl in class in my bare feet, but in spite of having to wear the compulsory school uniform, I had managed to incorporate my shoes from Rome with the Gucci bit and the stacked heels. This was as good a reason as any to get picked on by some of the wandering harridans in the corridors who cornered me to say they knew I had a father who was famous but they didn't know for what, and threatened to beat me up.

In the cold winter schoolyard, seated outside the music room window, I had spotted a small apple-cheeked girl with round horn-rimmed glasses. She was shielding her face with the lapel of her pea jacket and blowing smoke out through her sleeve. It billowed in the frosty air. She asked if I wanted a drag. It sounded like a pretty good idea. I took a puff of her cigarette and held the smoke in my mouth. Several other girls had gathered around. "Aren't you going to take it in?" one asked. Even after all the cigarettes Betts had shared with me, it had never occurred to me to inhale. "What do you mean?" I responded, and breathed in deeply. I almost fell over, I was so dizzy. The bell sounded and we dispersed for class. The following day, the same ritual happened, and this time Emily asked if I'd like to bunk off with her. "Skip school?" I asked. "It's only math," she said.

Emily Young quickly became my best friend. Her father was Wayland Hilton Young, 2nd Baron Kennet, a British writer and politician who served as chief whip of the Social Democratic Party in the House of Lords. He was the first parliamentarian to propose environmental laws, and had written the famous and daring book *Eros Denied,* a manifesto of the sexual revolution, which was causing something of a social stir among the older set.

Emily and I began a steady pattern of playing hooky. On Fridays, when Mum came home from the bank with cash for the week, she would put the white envelope inside a top drawer in her dresser. I would slip into her bedroom when she was out, or downstairs, and deftly swipe a couple of five-pound notes. I used the money to taxi back and forth to school. Once I'd arrive, I would walk into assembly, sign the register, then stroll out of the school gates with Emily to ponder the rest of the day.

Emily's eyes were startlingly blue, and when she took off her glasses, she'd blink at you like a baby, but she was the leader and made most of the decisions about where to go and what to do. Outside the grounds of Holland Park, Emily and I would roll our skirts up at the waist until they hit a point about eight inches above the knee, check ourselves out in the cracked mirror of a Max Factor compact, apply black pencil to the rims of our eyes, and dab Mary Quant white pearlized gloss on our lips.

Casually, we'd walk down the hill from Holland Park into Notting Hill Gate, stopping briefly to see what was playing at the Electric Cinema. They often imported movies from Italy and France, avant-garde stuff and documentaries. Then, onward to the Moulin Rouge Café, where we would order ice-cold Coca-Colas and smoke a few cigarettes. Sometimes the drummer Mick Fleetwood would come in with his brother-in-law, John Jesse, who owned an antique shop across the way, on Kensington Church Street. We never spoke to them; they were older than we were and the epitome of cool. I coveted an art nouveau pin in the window of John Jesse's shop, a cameo likeness of the actress Sarah Bernhardt, mounted in gold with opals, moonstones, and diamonds.

Down the street was the Lacquer Chest, an antique shop my mother favored, with an assortment of hardy-looking butcher's tables and rough-hewn furniture from the countryside. And a little farther down, round the bend toward Kensington High Street, was Biba's, the shoplifting mecca for teenage girls and the grooviest boutique in town. The interior of the store was deep plum, with drapings of black velvet, which provided ample opportunity for light fingers under the cover of darkness. We'd pore over the racks of dresses and stuff a few under our uniforms, and on the way out we'd check the velvet ottoman in the center of the floor to see if there were any rejects worthy of inclusion, waiting to be rehung.

Once we saw Cher and Sonny Bono get out of their limousine. She was wearing fur chaps and feathers and beads in her braids; we thought she looked amazing, like an Amazon ice queen. Everyone at school told me I looked like her, which pleased me a lot.

Later, in the nineties, I met Barbara Hulanicki, the creator of Biba, at a lunch. She reached for her pocketbook when the check came. I had to stop her. "No," I said, "I don't think you understand." But she did, and part of Barbara's genius was allowing us schoolgirls to get away with it—all the cutest girls in London were wearing her designs, and they were her best advertising.

Emily and I adopted a group of penniless hippies who occupied a basement under a fish-and-chip shop in Powis Terrace. They were the founding members of the London Free School, a disorganized group of hash-smoking dissidents, and we supported them by hitting up strangers for money around Notting Hill. Sometimes when our parents were out of town, we'd take them to our houses to bathe. The glut of filthy towels was occasionally difficult to explain, and my cat got a really bad reputation.

I had been home from a trip to Ireland for some days before and didn't know Mum was unaware that Nora Fitzgerald had died, quite suddenly, from cancer. When I made a reference to Nora's death, Mum burst into tears and asked how could I be so cold and uncaring as not to have told her. Was I made of stone? It hadn't occurred to me that no one had bothered to phone from Ireland to tell her Nora had been sick. It seemed to me that these days I found myself more at fault with Mum than ever before. Because she was unable to trust one word of my sloppy excuses, she resorted to interrogation. I was called to her room for a talking-to and forced to look her in the eye. Why had I lied about stealing Tony's sixpences? Was I smoking cigarettes? She could smell the tobacco on my clothes; she could see in my expression that I was lying to her. But when I think of it now, my parents were not being candid with me either.

Without missing a beat, I could meet Mum's gaze and swear that I'd kept my dental appointments with Dr. Endicott in Cavendish Square, the memory of his hairy knuckles in my mouth as visceral as if it had happened the day before (this was an era before dentists wore rubber gloves).

There was the recurring nightmare of not having taken the buttons to the local dressmaker, Miss Amshel, whom Mum had chosen to make up some clothes for me. In order to cover my tracks, I hid the buttons, some twenty or more, separately in drawers, pockets, under the carpet, in my bed. Like a trained retriever, Mum had tracked down each one to its hiding place, as I stood there, finally forced to blush and cry with shame, shaking my head as if denial were still an option.

John Julius Norwich was often at the house in the morning, doing the *Times* crossword puzzle with her. He lived directly across the canal, on Blomfield Road. Although he was genial, I didn't warm to him. He was obviously smart and interesting looking. He was titled (2nd Viscount Norwich) and was a historian, travel writer, and TV personality. He had very fine silvery hair and wore oval glasses. He wasn't anything like my father. But he and Mum seemed pretty cozy, having coffee at sunup, when I would come down to the kitchen for breakfast.

I was also a disappointing prospect to Miss Milner, a sweet elderly woman who had taught John Julius to play the piano in his youth. His influence on my mother, to my reasoning, was as good an excuse as any to resist learning even the simplest passage of music from his old teacher. Most of the lesson was spent beguiling Miss Milner into sharing her chocolate-covered digestive biscuits with me. I had honed my diversionary tactics years before on Mother Mary Borgia, at the convent in Loughrea, and they were now working effectively on Miss Milner.

In the summer of 1964 I went with the Spenders to their house in St. Jerôme, in Provence. My little black poodle, Mindy, had just died from kidney disease. My sadness at her loss was compounded with guilt at having been too lazy to walk her on school days and having left her in Ireland some months before. The house had no electricity, and on Saturday nights Lizzie and I danced with young, handsome Frenchmen wearing miniature Shetland sweaters in the village square.

Soon after I returned to London, I was in the car with Mum when she said, "Your father wants you and Tony to fly to Rome." My immediate response was "I don't want to go."

"Is it because of Zoë?" she asked. I thought that was weird—I hadn't seen Zoë, our beautiful Indian visitor, on the last couple of trips home to St. Clerans. She'd been out of the picture.

"No," I said. "I just don't want to go."

"Well," she said, "I think you have to."

Tony and I arrived in Rome a few days later. I was surprised when Betty opened the door to Dad's suite at the Grand Hotel. I wondered what she was doing there. She was wearing the three-quarter black mink jacket he had given her for Christmas that year. We entered the room. His back to the fireplace, Dad clapped his hands together as if scarcely able to contain his excitement. "Sit down, kids!" he commanded. Tony and I sat apart, stiffly, in wary expectation. "I've got some *great* news," said Dad. After a long dramatic pause, a heroic grin lit up his face. "You have a little brother!" he announced. It hung in the air for a moment like a dead fish.

I ran out of the suite into the nearest bathroom and locked the door. I was shaking. Finally I let Betty in and sobbed onto the shoulder of the mink jacket. "I hate him, I hate him."

Soon after, Tony and I got back into the car and were taken by Dad to a building in a gentrified part of town. We walked up some stairs to an apartment and Dad rang a bell. Zoë opened the door. Zoë, my friend. A small child was on all fours in the living room, barking. Dad thought it was hysterical that the toddler was acting like a dog, and kept telling him what a good little doggy he was. After a short time, we got up to go.

At the door, Zoë lifted the little boy and told him to kiss his brother, Tony. Tony gave him a kiss. Then came my turn; I looked at him with unconcealed hatred, and at under two years old, my baby brother, Danny, lifted his little hand and made a bear paw with it as he growled right back at me.

When Tony and I got back to London from Rome, something in the air had changed. Mum was sad. In the afternoon, I'd come home from school and find her crying in her room. On her bedside table was a bottle of Perrier and a glass, the jade horse's head, a notepad, a fountain pen, a stack of books—*Memories, Dreams, Reflections* by Carl Jung, and always something by Colette; she had given me *Chéri* to read when I turned thirteen. Mum had been advised by her therapist to write down all her dreams. I didn't really want to know why she was crying, or dare to ask. I knew I would not like the answer.

The school year was coming to an end when Mum said, "Anjelica, can't you make things easier on me? Can't you see I'm almost seven months pregnant?" I remember walking down by the canal with Lizzie, asking, "How? How could Mum be pregnant?"

There is a story that when she was in her third month and already showing an expanding waistline, Mum took a plane to Shannon and arrived at St. Clerans in time for afternoon drinks with the local priest. "I haven't seen my wife in a year," said Dad as she entered the room, to which she responded by flinging off her cloak in front of the assorted guests. I heard later that she and Dad had a terrible fight.

Divorces weren't nearly as acceptable then and were still practically unheard of in Ireland. Both my parents strayed during the marriage, and I think there was a sense, certainly on my father's part, that he was simply doing what came naturally to him. Probably with my mother, there was a bit of *You want to do that? I can do that, too.* Hoping, in a way, to get his attention. When she was in her late twenties she had affairs with quite a few men. There was a rumor about a brother of Aly Kahn, as well as an adventurer and scholar of Greek history, Paddy Leigh Fermor, who at eighteen walked the length of Europe from the Hook of Holland to Constantinople; Paddy was, I think, an important love in her life. I heard about her intervening between Paddy and another man at a party that turned into a big Irish brawl, both men drunk and about ready to kill each other, and Mum, in a white Dior gown, covered in blood. Later, Paddy worked on the screenplay for *The Roots of Heaven* with Dad.

I couldn't acknowledge the fact that my mother had lovers. Because to me, how could you even compare them with Dad? My father was a different cut. A swashbuckler, great-hearted and larger than life. He was intelligent and ironic, with a warm voice like whiskey and tobacco. I believe that without Dad to give shape to her existence, my mother didn't really know what to do or who to be. She must have been trepidatious, fearful of the future. Her father was rigorous, his demands on her so exacting that I think Mum had cultivated an aversion to failure. It translated easily into her relationship with Dad, who was considerably older, dominant, proud, and egotistical.

One imagines that life won't ever offer a decent alternative to the kind of high tension, expectations, and results of being with somebody like that. My father had a way of being dismissive that was quite devastating, of belittling people or ideas that he didn't feel were really up to par. I'm sure Mum was seeking something to overcome a feeling of inadequacy.

John Julius was pleasant to me, but I felt that he was cold and intellectual, and I was upset by the idea that this was the new love of my mother's life. I didn't know that he already had a wife, Anne. I desperately wanted my parents to be together. Evidently, now, this would never happen. I had asked Mum, "How can you call other men 'darling' but never Dad?" And she told me that sometimes, when people grew up, they also grew apart. The details of our parents' separation went largely unexplained, but Tony and I knew how loaded it was. It scared and worried me. Although Tony and I didn't talk about it, I knew he missed the old Dad, the one who spoiled us as children.

When John Julius didn't get a divorce and marry Mum, and it became obvious that she was going to have his baby by herself, I think her heart was broken. And as I understand it now, my mother wasn't John Julius's only port of call.

Mum told me that when she was pregnant with Allegra, John Julius's mother, Lady Diana Cooper, had come by the house with a bunch of violets. Mum was ambivalent about the gesture, feeling there was something condescending about it, particularly in Diana's choice of flowers, like a bouquet a grand person might present to a poor relation, she said.

On August 26, Allegra was born. And on the third day home from the hospital, when I looked at this perfect infant with her rosebud mouth, asleep in her crib in Mum's room, I leaned down and kissed her and instantly fell in love. Allegra as a baby had a round head, wispy pale blond hair, big slate-blue eyes, and a grave, slightly imperious countenance that reminded us of an infant Queen Victoria. She called me "Kika." Mum used to love to dress her in antique linens and lace, and after her bath time Nurse would bring her downstairs in full regalia, smelling of shampoo and baby powder, before putting her to bed.

Dad stood alone. He was a lonesome pine. I think there were places that my father wouldn't go with anyone. He had demons. He could be charming and captivating, seductive and charismatic, but if he had it in for you, watch out. His eyes were brown and inquisitive, like monkeys' eyes, with a keen intelligence. But when he got angry, they would turn red. He was disgusted by ignorance, prejudice, and stupidity, but sometimes I think that Dad was just plain angry, and vodka fueled that rage.

The only book my father read to Tony and me was *Old Yeller,* a heartbreaker that I doubt I ever recovered from. One of his favorite conversational gambits was to question our knowledge of rarefied information over dinner, such as "Where does lightning come from? Below or above?" I always felt put on the spot, Dad's eyebrow raised for an extended moment, in which I made the mistake of groping for the answer. Or he would lay out playful—if controversial—theories, such as that everyone in the world should be allowed to kill three others over a lifetime.

Dad was apt to declare preordained decisions about what would be best for our futures. That Tony should enter the minefield of Irish politics, even though he had hitherto shown no particular interest in that arena, rather preferring the more solitary and aesthetic pursuits of falconry and music. Or that, now, at the age of fourteen, I was to have my life in Ireland and London supplanted by art studies at L'Ecole du Louvre, in Paris. It had not occurred to him that this idea was no less than horrifying to me in light of the miseries I had suffered at the Lycée.

When he summoned me to his room for that particular discussion, I reacted so badly to his proposal that he questioned my sanity. Whenever Dad put me on the spot, I became at first quiet and then defensive, and then, more often than not, I left his room in tears. Lately, the only way to please Dad, I felt, would be to sacrifice my own choices in life to make him happy. Dad criticized the way I dressed, my use of makeup, the fact that I now smoked.

On the night before Christmas Eve 1965, a few of us were dancing in the drawing room. The actor Patrick O'Neal, who was preparing to do *The Kremlin Letter* with Dad, was visiting with his wife, Cynthia. I guess he said something to Dad about my moving provocatively, because in the morning I got an ominous phone call from Betty, saying, "Come up to the Big House. Your father wants to see you in his room."

I could not imagine what I had done, but I was anxious. I walked up the driveway with dread in my heart. When I entered his room, Dad told me to sit down. "I have it on good authority that you were doing the bumps last night," he said.

I had never before heard the expression. "What are the bumps?" I asked.

"You know damn well what the bumps are," he said, turning aside.

I asked again, "What are the bumps, Dad?" By now it was starting to dawn on me that moving my hips in a certain way—that was the bumps. I began to protest. He told me to be quiet. I started to cry. "You don't love me," I said defiantly. Suddenly, his arm swung back and his hand hit me hard in the face, backward and forward; the force of it was like walking into a wall.

As soon as my vision cleared, I ran out of his room as fast as I could, charged downstairs and across the gravel yard, and flew down the driveway to the Little House, choking on my tears. I was crying so hard I couldn't breathe. I was hysterical. Tony found me and wet some towels with cold water and put them on my head and neck to try to calm me down. Tony could be a bully, but if anyone else attempted to hurt or take advantage of me, he always came to my rescue and valiantly tried to comfort me.

The "bumps" problem was an anomaly. Generally, Dad loved that I was athletic and that I could stand on my head or that I could bend my spine and rock my entire body like a boat. He thought that was just wonderful, though obviously not to the point of my being seductive.

After that episode, I avoided Dad assiduously. On Christmas Day we were all clustered around the tree. We had not spoken. I'd bought him a beautiful present, a Claddagh chieftain's brooch from a trip to Dublin, an old one that I'd found at Louis Wine's antique shop. I think he was ashamed. He said "Thank you" sheepishly, and bent to kiss me. I didn't want to be near him, I didn't want to be around him. He scared me.

Tony was kind when Dad got tough with me. And Dad was certainly no easier on Tony. Tony got sent from the dining table with alarming regularity, for small infringements that became magnified by defensiveness on his part. The more guarded and stoic Tony became, the more punishing Dad could be. I was targeted at lunch for declaring that I did not like the artist Van Gogh. Dad said, "Name me five Van Gogh paintings and you can stay; otherwise, leave the room."

Dad had given Tony some Native American deerskin jackets, which Tony had adopted as his falconry uniform. All day long, throughout the holidays, he was carrying his hawks around, his chest covered in blood, scat, feathers, and guts. When he appeared in this condition for lunch in Dad's absence, no one at the Big House had much to say. Tony did as he pleased. But when he made the mistake of doing so in front of Dad, he was severely humiliated in front of everyone. There was a pattern developing around these infractions. The offenses were repeated and they occurred with greater frequency. The accompanying words of admonishment from Dad rose in volume according to his frustration, and before you knew it, it felt like war was being waged between them in the dining room.

In the summer of 1965, I went to Saint-Jean-Cap-Ferrat with Joan and her parents for three weeks. There was a mistral and it rained most of the time, which in France, we had heard, meant that if you committed a crime you could get off with a light sentence. The actor Jack Hawkins was living next door to the Bucks, and I had a crush on his youngest son, Andy. We listened to popular French songs like "Quand un bateau passe," by Claude François, and "Tous les garçons," by Françoise Hardy. In the mornings, we'd dive off the end of the dock into deep blue water. The Mediterranean was not so polluted in those days; all the seafood came from there and not from Chile.

I longed to fall in love and I was just starting to understand my power. When Joan gave a party, I spent most of the evening speaking in French to a poetic-looking blond boy much older than I. He invited me to a dinner at his villa later that week, but he wasn't around when Joan and I arrived, and we didn't know anyone there, so we left.

When I returned to England, Emily told me that she had been going out with Mayo Elstob, Joshua's friend from Town and Country. I thought this would make for a good opportunity to meet up with Joshua again, as we had lost contact. Emily came over on a Saturday night with both of them, and we went upstairs to my room. I turned off the lights and lit the candles in the candelabra.

It was very beautiful in the dusk, so we decided to go up to Hampstead Heath and smoke banana peel instead; someone said it might get you high. It didn't work, and we spent the evening wandering back down from the heath to Emily's parents' house on the Bayswater Road.

I called Mum and asked if I could stay over at Emily's. She said yes. That night, Joshua came into my bed, but I was suddenly turned off by his reciprocity. He was urgent and confessional and told me that he had cared for me even while I was pining for him at Town and Country.

In the early-morning hours, we got up and went for a sad walk in Hyde Park. Joshua told me he had stomach cramps. We said goodbye. I never saw him again.

Mum had taken me to Venice for the first time in 1961 to see an exhibition of the fifteenth-century painter Vittore Carpaccio at the Doge's Palace. I fell in love with the city as soon as I laid eyes on it—a soft, shimmering view across the Grand Canal to the Piazza San Marco, with its two columns topped by gold-winged lions, rising like a miracle out of the sea. The pictures were fantastic; I loved a portrait of Saint Ursula, asleep, with her cheek cupped in the palm of her hand. Mum loved the delicate little flowers and shrubs that grew in the crevices of the parterre in the paintings. I could feel her gearing up to re-create this visual in the garden at Maida Avenue.

The next time we went to Venice, she invited Emily to come with us. Our rooms were on the Grand Canal, at the Gritti Palace, and when we drew the curtains and flung open the shutters, which had been closed for the night, the early sun streamed in and the reflection of the water below danced on the ceiling of our bright red room. The gondoliers sang songs like Grandpa used to sing, and the prows of their boats, slicing through the silvery stillness of the lagoon, looked like seabirds arching their necks.

Mum had met a woman in Venice on a previous trip, someone she found very fascinating, an artist whose name was Manina. On our way to her apartment, we walked across several bridges and waterfront pavements to a chorus of wolf whistles. The Italian men loved Emily and were always trying to pinch her bottom. She was very sanguine about this—in those days one didn't think of it as sexual harassment but rather as just something that happened to you, especially if you were young or pretty or voluptuous. On the contrary, one was just a little flattered.

Turning the corner of a busy pedestrian thoroughfare onto a relatively quiet street, Mum paused for a moment and said, "Look! There she is! She always knows when I'm coming, even when I haven't called first—that's why she's waiting downstairs!"

Manina was small and delicately made, with huge dark eyes lined in kohl and a direct gaze. She took us upstairs to her dim apartment and gave us lemonade. Her drawings of great glowering birds adorned with colored glass hung on the walls. She was creating amulets by melting lead into liquid in a saucepan and decorating the molten metal with glass beads from Murano. Then Manina introduced us all to the I Ching, and Mum, Emily, and I threw our coins.

Across the canal, in another deserted palazzo, lived a Cuban friend of Mum's, an artist called Domingo de la Cueva. He showed us some of his work, mostly jewelry—breastplates, armbands, and circlets. The most impressive piece was a girdle of fire opals, rough rubies, diamonds, shells, and semiprecious stones, all set in rose gold. He told us he was incapable of leaving Venice, even for a holiday. "I feel I will die without her," he said. "Every time I try to leave, I get sick. I feel as if I am never going to see my city again."

We went for Bellinis at Harry's Bar and had lunch on the nearby island of Torcello. We went across the bay to Murano to see glass being blown; on the beach outside the factory, the sand was strewn with colored pebbles. I collected some for future amulets of my own.

A few days later, we went to visit Grandpa, who was vacationing at his birthplace on Lago Maggiore. As we drove across the Veneto to the lakes, Mum taught Emily and me the "Sorrow" song. Emily and I loved to harmonize together, although she had a much better voice than I.

> *O she was a lass from the low country,*
> *And he was a Lord of high degree,*
> *And she loved his Lordship so tenderly.*
> *O Sorrow!*
> *Sing Sorrow!*
> *Now she sleeps in the valley, where the wildflowers nod,*
> *And no one knew she loved him,*
> *But herself and God.*

In the tiny town of Ispra, near Varese on Lago Maggiore, we visited Mum's family, living very traditionally in a simple but handsome house. They served us lunch; we must have been thirty people—teenagers, aunts, uncles, grandmas, babies. And most precious of all, dressed in black from head to toe, my grandpa's eldest sister, my great-aunt Agnèsé, a woman as tiny and wrinkled and old and beautiful as we had ever seen.

CHAPTER 11

John and Anjelica on the set
of *Sinful Davey*, 1968

mily and I went to some great concerts—the Four Tops,
Steve Winwood and Jim Capaldi in Traffic, Cream, the
Yardbirds, the Kinks, Jeff Beck, John Mayall, Eric Burdon and
the Animals, singing "House of the Rising Sun." We favored
the Rolling Stones, especially Mick and Keith. There were live

clubs all over London, and you could go out to Chalk Farm or Eel Pie Island to hear new groups. And in the coffeehouses, Bert Jansch or Nina Simone would be playing.

At the Royal Albert Hall in summertime, they would hold the proms, and as a student you could get in to watch beautiful concerts for free, up near the dome, "in the Gods." These new tape recorders had just come out in America that you could sling over your shoulder and have sounds wherever you went. All of a sudden, music was everywhere. A sound track for your life.

We would go to Powis Terrace and listen to Pink Floyd rehearse in the church hall, and to Earls Court to see Jimi Hendrix make love to his guitar onstage, plucking the strings with his teeth as she wailed for him. I wore a pink satin dress with printed flowers and a straw hat with a big brim and a long blue satin ribbon. I rode a carousel next to the stage, dizzily, for hours.

These were the days of *Room at the Top, Darling,* Antonioni's *Blow-Up, Georgy Girl, The Servant, Girl with the Green Eyes, Privilege,* and the Nouvelle Vague filmmakers—Jean-Luc Godard, François Truffaut, Eric Rohmer, Louis Malle, Claude Chabrol. *Jules et Jim, Alphaville, Les enfants du paradis, La belle et la bête*—I went to all these movies with my mother. The sound track of *A Man and a Woman* was always on the record player. I loved Anouk Aimée, because she wore her hair parted on the side over one eye in the movie and looked a lot like Mum. I remember being very upset after seeing *La peau douce,* a Truffaut film, with the actress Françoise Dorléac. I think it was because I found her so devastatingly beautiful, or because the leading man, Jean Desailly, was ugly with pockmarked skin, and the movie was strange and dark and sexual. *Ready, Steady, Go* and *Top of the Pops* were our favorite TV music shows, and I loved the American series—*The Fugitive, Dr. Kildare,* and the cowboys in *Bonanza.*

The women of this time were singular beauties, at parties, clubs, walking down the Kings Road, wearing crochet caps, mink from the twenties, and see-through chiffon. There was a medley of breathtaking English roses—girls like Jill Kennington, Sue Murray, Celia Hammond, the indelibly beautiful Jean Shrimpton, and Pattie Boyd, who later married George Harrison. Jane Birkin, a rock-and-roll virgin with a gap between her teeth, who ran off with Serge Gainsbourg and sang the breathy "Je t'aime, moi non plus." There were fantastic actresses breaking out on the scene, like Maggie Smith, Sarah Miles, Susannah York, Vanessa Redgrave and her sister, Lynn. The French beauties—Delphine Seyrig, Catherine Deneuve, Anna Karina. The ingénues—Judy Geeson, Hayley Mills, Jane Asher, Rita Tushingham. The American Jane Fonda as Barbarella. Marsha Hunt, with her crowning afro. The singers—the great Dusty Springfield; Cilla Black; the barefoot Sandie Shaw; cool, tall Françoise Hardy; and the bleached-blond Sylvie Vartan. The rock-goddess Julie Driscoll, whose interview with British *Vogue,* which began, "When I wake up in the morning my breath smells like a gorilla's armpit," was memorably descriptive. I remember thinking this woman was not out to impress the opposite sex.

The scents of London in the sixties—Vetiver, Brut, and Old Spice for the boys; lavender, sandalwood, and Fracas for the girls; unwashed hair, cigarettes. Along the Portobello Road, fish and chips and vinegar, tobacco, patchouli, curry, freshly rotting fruit, bacon frying, a trace of body odor. The pubs would be spilling onto the sidewalks by lunchtime, everyone drinking cider and beer, football on the television. Up and down the Kings Road, the beauties in rumpled silk and denim would be out in force on Saturday afternoons. Playful exotics blooming all around in eighteenth-century frock coats—girls with faces like cameos. The blond temptresses Elke Sommer and Brigitte Bardot paving the way for the soulful beauty of Marianne Faithfull and Keith Richards's dangerous German, Anita Pallenberg. The press called them Dolly Birds, but they were predatory— the sirens of modern sin.

The guys wore bell-bottoms and velvet jackets, the cuffs dripping with lace; the girls had kohl-rimmed eyes, long straight hair, Afghani embroidered jerkins, printed dresses, military accessories, fingerless gloves, lace-up boots, bird feathers and monkey fur, high-collared Russian shirts, and miniskirts up to there. I found a drummer-boy's jacket in red felt with gold braid that looked like something out of *Sgt. Pepper's,* and wore it with tea gowns from the thirties and pale straw hats with wide brims beaded and feathered, a ring on every finger, earrings hanging to my collarbone.

On the Sundays we stayed in town, Mum would cook an afternoon pork roast with crackling on top, fresh baked apples with cloves and cinnamon, roasted potatoes, and a big salad, Italian-style. Ten to twelve people sat down at the bleached-pine dining table in the kitchen, with the French doors open to the garden. Nurse would carry Allegra downstairs after her bath to kiss everyone good night. There was usually the core group of Mum's friends—Peter Menegas, the Bucks, the O'Tooles, Gina Medcalf, and Leslie Waddington, whom Mum had recently asked to be Allegra's godfather. Tony Richardson came often, with his partner, Neil Hartley, as did the actor Peter Eyre, the costume designer Bumble Dawson, Dirk Bogarde, the director Joseph Losey, and the artist Eduardo Paolozzi. And there were American friends who had just arrived in town, or sent their protégés over for Mum's protection. She loved mixing up ages and nationalities at her table.

When Diana Sands came to the West End, starring in *The Great White Hope* with James Earl Jones, she had introduced Mum to her friend the playwright Adrienne Kennedy. And when Goddard Lieberson's son, Jonathan, came to London, Mum immediately included him on the calendar of events and took a shine to his good friend Penelope Tree, even though she was the daughter of Marietta, a longtime rival for Dad's affections. Mum must have realized by then that there was little any woman could do to hold Dad's attention. Many years later I was to become the godmother to Penelope's daughter, Paloma.

The great fashion photographer Richard Avedon was a friend of my parents. I don't know if it was his or Mum's idea that he should photograph me. I posed for him at a studio off the Fulham Road in Chelsea. I was very shy and, true to form, I applied a lot of makeup. He told Mum later that my shoulders were too wide and that he very much doubted I would ever be a model.

Some guys from NASA came to Holland Park. Their models and maquettes were mounted outside the auditorium in the assembly hall. There were big signs on them saying "Do Not Touch," and we were warned that they cost a lot of money. In assembly, our headmaster, a humorless man prone to outbursts of rage, asked the students if we had any questions for the guys from NASA. I rose to my feet and asked why we were sending people into space when we couldn't feed the world. I was told to sit down and be quiet. It's a question that still bothers me.

On a school holiday in August 1966, I went to stay with the Bucks again for a few weeks at their rented house, Villa la Gabbia, in Saint-Jean-Cap-Ferrat. Returning to London through Paris, I went shopping with Joan and Joyce and bought a brown wool suit with a Nehru collar at a boutique called Snob's on the rue de Berri. Joan took me to see *Tartuffe* at the Comédie-Française. After dinner one night we went to Castel's, the happening nightclub, and I received a lot of attention from some old French playboys, which aggravated Joan enormously. I was taller and looked older than she did, and I was wearing makeup and a miniskirt.

Betts introduced me to some Irish boys later that summer. She had invited them to come down for the Galway races. All three young men wore the classic uniform of the gentry—Harris Tweed jacket, beige twill trousers, brown felt trilby, and tan lace-up shoes with a high polish. Betts said, "This is Mikey." I blushed as I shook his hand. Mikey was nineteen or twenty. Betts had described him as her favorite godson and told me that his father owned an estate called Mount Juliet in Co. Kilkenny. He was fine-boned, brown-haired, slight, of medium height, with kind eyes. He had a little scar, either at the corner of his eye or on his upper lip. He was using crutches and looked like a young soldier come back from the war. One leg was in plaster; he had broken it recently in a riding accident. He and his friends stayed for three days, during which I fell more deeply in his thrall. Betts had also invited two girls, the Harboards, daughters of racing friends of hers, to come down from the Curragh, in Co. Kildare, and round out the numbers. The boys were to occupy the loft and the girls the Little House.

On the last night of their stay, after the races, we went to a dance at the Great Southern Hotel on Eyre Square, where a predominantly céilí band played a cover of a popular song by the Seekers titled, not inappropriately, "The Carnival Is Over." Outside on the green, the buskers who ran the flying chairs, the carousel, and the bumper cars were packing up until the next year.

When we returned to the Little House, Mikey came up to my bedroom. We lay down on my little four-poster bed and he held me in his arms. My heart was beating loud and fast, and the heavy inanimate weight of the plaster cast was like a wall between us. We never even kissed. We stayed frozen in silence for a short while, then he went to join his friends in the loft across the courtyard. The following morning, he left with them to go back up to Dublin.

I was sad when he left. Betty gave me a photograph of him, atop a tall chestnut, wearing jockey silks. Later, she showed me the letters she'd received from all three boys, dutifully thanking her for the outing to Galway. There was no mention of me in any of them.

Dad had met Carson McCullers during the war when he was visiting Paulette Goddard and Burgess Meredith in upstate New York. She was already very fragile, having survived the first in a series of strokes in her thirties. Twenty years later, Dad and Ray Stark decided to make McCullers's *Reflections in a Golden Eye*, and chose the Scottish novelist Chaplin Mortimer to write the screenplay. In September 1966, after Carson had read the script, Dad went to discuss it with her at her home in Nyack, New York. As they sat sipping bourbon, Dad suddenly invited Carson to St. Clerans, not thinking for an instant that she might accept. But she told him she would come to visit the following February, when he would have wrapped work on *Reflections*.

Dad picked Carson up from Shannon Airport in an ambulance; she was in the company of her devoted companion, Ida Reeder, a sweet, cheerful black woman. When they arrived at

St. Clerans, Carson requested a tour. Her stretcher was carried from room to room as she asked questions about each object's history and each painting's provenance. After she was settled in a hospital bed in the Grey Room, Carson's head was just a tiny round skull above the sheets; she was half doll, half mouse; her transparent shoulders melted into the pillows. There was no discernible shape of a body, save for a delicate little hand, white as porcelain, that held fast to a silver stirrup cup. Tony and I stood at her bedside as she absorbed us with enormous eyes, like blotting paper.

She never left the Grey Room for the remainder of the visit. Soon she departed as she had arrived, in the ambulance. She died just a few months later, leaving the little silver cup to my father, engraved "John Love Carson, 1967."

When Marlon Brando came to St. Clerans to see Dad before starting work on *Reflections in a Golden Eye,* there was great excitement among the girls in the kitchen. They were squeezing orange juice in their eyes to make them bright, and their updos, stiff with hair spray, lasted from Friday all the way through to Monday.

I went up to the Big House one morning and found a tanned, even-featured man in a maroon velour sweatshirt standing on the upstairs landing, talking to Dad, who introduced me to him. Marlon smiled and his lips curled. He spoke through his nose. That afternoon in the study, Marlon gave me a tortoiseshell ring from Tahiti, inlaid with silver, and asked me if I'd like to visit him there someday. Later he went for a walk in a lashing horizontal rain, and Betts and I went out in the car to search for him. Finally, we located Marlon, staggering along against the wind on the dirt road near the Sarsfield Bridge, but he refused Betts's offer of a lift.

Burgess Meredith came to stay from California. We all loved "Buzz." He had a deep gravelly voice and a great sense of humor. He was a good rider and loved hunting with the Galway Blazers. Betts found him a beautiful chestnut mare he called Kinvara, which he shipped back to America when he went home.

Dad made a film called *Sinful Davey* in Ireland in 1968. It starred John Hurt, with a supporting cast that included Nigel Davenport and Robert Morley. They were filming at Leenane, in the wilds of Connemara. Cherokee Habe had a production job on the movie. Because Mum was in London and Cherokee's daughter, Marina, was now in college at the University of Hawaii, Cherokee and I gravitated to each other. Cherokee was a great-looking woman with a shock of platinum-blond hair, tanned skin, and Native American features. She was fun to hang out with. Although I was just a teenager and she was in her late forties, Cherokee became my best friend on the set of *Sinful Davey*. She shared confidences with me. I had a crush on the leading man, John Hurt, and she was having a set romance with Nigel Davenport. I did some day work riding sidesaddle in a hunt for the film; otherwise, I was a little bored hanging out with the cast in the evenings.

Betty arranged for me to go up to the Curragh, to stay with the Harboard girls. I went to several race meets with them, and everywhere we went, I hoped I might run into Mikey. Then Carol, the elder sister, told me he was seeing an American girl.

When the film crew moved to Dublin, I started going to the hunt balls and staying out late, which upset Dad. I think he half-expected me to stay in my room at night. I went to the Dublin Horse Show and finally re-met Mikey McCalmont, who barely gave me the time of day.

Toward the end of filming, I had a brief and disillusioning episode with the son of Dad's production manager. Darkly handsome, in his early twenties, he came to my room after a party at the Gresham Hotel. I was wearing false eyelashes and a fall. The encounter was unpleasant, in that he attempted unsuccessfully to force me to give him pleasure. He was completely insensitive, like an immutable force. When I woke up to a trail of false eyelashes, fake hair, and push-up bra, I felt like Paddy Lynch's song "Oh Wasn't She Charming for Nineteen Years Old." I was not yet seventeen.

Back at school, I had developed a crush on the brother of one of the girls in my class, Joe, a handsome boy who had left Holland Park the year before and was often seen in the neighborhood wearing a black policeman's cape. One afternoon found four of us together at a bleak bed-sit on the Harrow Road. The other couple disappeared to a room next door. Suddenly confronted with the object of my desire, I found the consequent attempt at lovemaking disastrous, love having nothing to do with it. After a hasty, fumbling effort, he rose from the bed to make a strawberry-jam sandwich on white bread. I was ashamed and embarrassed. I left and waited at a bus stop on the Harrow Road. A dirty old man showed me crude pencil drawings of women in compromising positions. I tried to ignore him.

Emily's parents discovered that she was skipping classes with me. We were separated and she was sent to Saffron Walden, a Quaker boarding school in Essex. My friend from Town and Country, Anne Rothenstein, agreed to go with me to see Emily during visitors' weekend. I had told Mum that I was staying at Anne's house in North London. We traveled down to Essex several hours by train, fully meaning to make it back to town that night. The boarding school was very depressing—Emily showed me a row of cigarette butts she had lined up outside the windowsill of a room she shared with another girl. Anne and I were supposed to leave early and catch the train back to London, but we lingered and were caught later trying to sleep over in the cloakroom by one of the teachers and asked to leave the school grounds. I can't remember how we got home, but by some miracle Mum didn't find out. She had gone to Oslo, Norway, with Nurse and Allegra to visit her friend Richard Svara.

Soon after my visit with Emily, I went on a trip to Los Angeles with Mum. Cherokee and Marina met us at the airport at the top of the elevator by the arrivals gate. Marina was not as tall as I was, but ever since our Christmas at St. Clerans as children, when we played the three witches and she wore the red flannel nightgown that said "don't tease me," I'd thought she was one of the most beautiful girls I had ever seen.

At seventeen, she still had long blond hair and was sloe-eyed, with graceful, delicate features. We laughed about how obsessed I'd been with her Barbie dolls years before. I don't remember seeing her again before Mum and I went back to London.

Mum told me later that on December 29, 1968, Marina was brutally murdered on Mulholland Drive in Los Angeles. She had come back to California for a vacation and one evening had gone to see her boyfriend and stayed out late. After driving home, she was abducted in the driveway of Cherokee's house at 3:30 A.M. Her killer was never identified.

Around this time, Joan and I had a temporary falling-out because Dad and her father, Jules, had undergone an irreparable work-related breach and become estranged. But this in no way affected Joan's deep affection for Mum, nor my love for Jules and Joyce.

A school search was being launched for a girl for Franco Zeffirelli's *Romeo and Juliet.* I had talked to one of the producers, Dyson Lovell, when he came to Holland Park, and he wanted me to audition. But that summer, in Ireland, it became clear that Dad had other plans for me. Having completed the first movie in a three-picture deal for Fox, he had decided that the second would be the film to launch me as an actress. I wasn't sure I wanted to do it. It was called *A Walk with Love and Death.* When I read the script, I didn't connect with the role. I thought the dialogue was corny, and, more important, I was still uncomfortable and wary around Dad. When I returned to London, I talked to Mum about it—she seemed concerned and sympathetic, but I don't think she wanted to confront Dad with this indecision and insecurity any more than I did. She said, "He wants you to do it. He's doing it for you. I think you're going to have to do it." Dad consequently wrote a letter to Zeffirelli, telling him that I was unavailable for the part of Juliet.

I would have much preferred to work with Zeffirelli. The prospect of making a movie with Dad, his directing me, surrounded by his regular crew, most of whom had known me since babyhood—Basil Fenton-Smith on sound, script supervisor Angela Allen, the lighting cameraman Ed Scaife, Russ Lloyd in the cutting room—would diminish my power to self-invent on my own terms. It was as important for me to present a new persona off-camera as it was to play an original character on film.

CHAPTER 12

Anjelica at home,
British *Vogue,* December 1967

On country weekends in England, house parties would assemble for friends to share living quarters, go to the races, have lovely meals, play tennis, do a little gardening, wander with the dogs in the local fields and woods, ride on horseback, visit other friends for Bloody Marys or Pimm's Cups, drive to the beach, and eat delicious Sunday roasts with Yorkshire pudding.

Mum and I often went to Dirk Bogarde and Tony Forwood's beautiful old farmhouse in Kent. Before lunch, the usual party of smart, attractive, sophisticated people—from Joe Losey to Boaty Boatwright, then a top executive at Universal, and her husband, the producer Terence Baker, to Bumble Dawson, the actors Georgia Brown, Roddy McDowall, and Michael York, to Jean Kennedy Smith and Sybil Burton—would gather in the bright living room with its pastel sofas and chintz pillows, its bowls of pink roses and bluebells, to talk about art and theater and movies and books.

It was there that Mum met the actor James Fox, twenty-eight years old, a tall, blond, remarkably handsome, Harrow-educated British movie star. Everyone called him Willy. His father was the famous theatrical agent Robin Fox. Willy was working with Dirk on a film called *The Servant,* directed by Joe Losey. One night he came to Maida Avenue for dinner, and I felt him appraising me—sizing me up. I was seventeen, and I looked back. I was wearing a chocolate-brown velvet dress with a lace collar that I'd found at Antiquarius. I was aware that I looked fetching. I heard him tell Mum he thought I was beautiful.

Later that week, she came to my room and said, "Willy Fox wants to take you to dinner. I'm not sure if I should let you go." I said, "Oh, Mum, please. I'll be good." And she said, "All right." I think she had a word with him too; quite honestly, she must have felt that if it was not going to be her, at least it would be me. So she consented.

Willy took me to a small house in Belgravia, in a mews called Three Kings Yard. That night, I met his friends the actress Deborah Dixon and the director Donald Cammell. I thought they were the coolest, most attractive, most seductive people. A joint was passed around and we ate lamb stew. Willy drove me home and kissed me. We arranged for him to pick me up during school hours the following day; it was to be our secret.

He had a new purple Lotus Elan, the color of the red cabbage leaf he'd given as a sample for the custom paint job. As we drove out to the country, he put a tape in the machine, and for the first time in my life I heard Otis Redding. We had lunch at the home of the production designer for his new film, *Isadora*. Afterward, when we returned to London, he took me back to Three Kings Yard and made love to me. Thus began a short series of after-school visits, none lasting longer than a few hours. I had taken to getting myself to Belgravia as well, so I was waiting for him one afternoon alone in his apartment when Donald Cammell walked in from next door. "What are you doing here alone? Come keep me company. Let's have a smoke."

Whatever it was he gave me, everything went sideways. Donald Cammell was a dangerous man. I don't know what he said to Willy, but when I saw Willy next, he said, "Did Donald go after you? What was he thinking? You're my girlfriend." But I wasn't. He had a girlfriend—Andee Cohen, an American he'd met months before. I heard from Mum that she was coming to London and that Willy was meeting her at the airport. Mum had no idea that Willy and I had slept together. I began to dread seeing Mum's little silver car parked outside 31 Maida Avenue. It meant she'd be home. That she'd ask questions, require answers.

Andee looked like a Gernreich model, with a Vidal Sassoon haircut—pretty and stick thin. She and Willy were obviously very much in love and demonstrative in public. I remember going to a lunch with Mum at Leslie Waddington's apartment and Willy and Andee disappearing into a bedroom directly afterward. I never confronted him.

The winter before, I had gone to Klosters and stayed with the Viertels. One day, I found myself in a blizzard at the top of the Graubünden alpine range with Peter, and we almost got lost in the whiteout; he kept his humor and didn't falter, but I could see he had a moment's pause, blind in the freezing cold. That night, I met a handsome young man in a floor-length wolf coat whose name was Baron Arnaud de Rosnay. He was a photographer and was dating Marisa Berenson. I danced with him at the disco in town. Percy Sledge was singing "When a Man Loves a Woman." Before I left Switzerland, we had exchanged telephone numbers. Now Arnaud had broken up with Marisa and wanted to come to London to take my photograph for British *Vogue*.

When he arrived at the house, my mother took one look at Arnaud and thought he was fabulous. She couldn't understand that I wanted nothing to do with him; Mum and I posed for him, walking together in Irish capes along the bank of the Regents Canal. It was a nice day, but I didn't even invite him to stay over for dinner. Willy Fox had broken my heart.

One morning as I was getting into a taxicab on Maida Avenue with Mum, I felt a sharp, stabbing pain in my lower abdomen. I must have temporarily turned white, because she noticed and was concerned, asking if I was all right. I answered that yes, I was. I did not want her to take me to a doctor to get examined. The truth would come out—that I was only seventeen and already having sex would be shocking to her—and she would tell Dad and all hell would break loose. So when the pain recurred, again I said nothing. Eventually, it went away and I thought no more about it.

I loved Deborah Dixon's haircut. It curled at the nape of her neck like the marble portrait of a young Greek boy. I decided I wanted to look like her. So off I went to Vidal Sassoon, but only weeks before I was due to start work on *A Walk with Love and Death.*

Dad was seriously displeased and saw this as a sign of rebellion, sure that I had chopped off my hair as some form of protest. But the truth was, I didn't want to do the film, and I hadn't reckoned on its coming to fruition in any way.

Mum took me shopping and bought me a yellow wool suit that we hoped Dad would like. Days later, as I was fretting about an acting debut I did not want to make, I got a call from British *Vogue* asking me to pose for my first portrait with David Bailey. At this point, modeling was much more alluring to me than acting in a movie for Dad. It was remarkable how things came so easily to me. In every generation a flock of pretty girls was released into society with the help of their mothers, via the pages of the glamour magazines. They wore the bright plumage of the newly initiated, and the adornments of their ancestors only served to enhance their youth. Often they were the progeny of good bloodlines—rich, clever, famous fathers and the beautiful women who married them. I was no exception to this fortunate rule, but in retrospect I remember wishing I had something to fight for. This was the beginning of a habit of making things harder for myself than they needed to be.

The first time I had seen Bailey was across a crowded room at a cocktail party in Jules and Joyce Buck's flat in Belgravia when I was twelve and he was in his late twenties. He was not tall but seemed physically strong—that is to say, he filled his jeans. He was wearing a black leather jacket and black stack-heeled cowboy boots. He had black eyes and shaggy black hair. Beside him, in a soft pink ultra-minidress, with long pale gold hair, sat the ravishing Catherine Deneuve. I was introduced to them as a child is introduced to grown-ups. I can still see them, like day and night across the room—light and dark, her cool and his intensity.

His reputation, of course, preceded him. Bailey was known to have been the discoverer and lover and photographer of the other most beautiful woman in the world, Jean Shrimpton, who was living with the handsomest man in the world, Terence Stamp. I had passed them walking toward the Albany in Picca-dilly once, and had literally gasped at their collective radiance; she, with her doe eyes, perfect pout, and pointed little chin, was hanging on his arm. Many of the iconic photographs of the day were Bailey's. Then Penelope Tree became his girlfriend. I had seen them come out of an elevator once in Paris. She was an amazing-looking girl, with endless legs in thigh-high boots and no hips at all. Her eyes were widely spaced, with a distant expression, like those of a beautiful insect.

I'd been in the dressing room for hours, trying without success to learn the knack of applying individual lashes to the lower lids. Glue was everywhere, my eyes were a sticky mess, I was on the verge of tears. Celia Hammond, my favorite model of the moment, popped her head with its mane of silky blond hair through the doorway to say goodbye to the editor. She was even more exquisite in the flesh than in her photographs. As the door closed, I was left in her wake as if the sun had disappeared behind a cloud. I was out of my league. It was dark in the studio except for the blinking of a strobe light under a silver umbrella. Against the wall, a sheet of gray no-seam paper was suspended from the ceiling.

Bailey looked me up and down and said cheerfully, "Hello, missy."

I felt both nervous and defensive. "Please don't call me that," I said coolly.

Bailey took my picture in a version of the haute gypsy look that Marisa Berenson and Penelope Tree had made popular—with eyes like starfish. I faced the lens warily, as if it were a dog about to bite. But Bailey seemed not too concerned with my negativity. He clicked off a few rolls and that was it. The end of the session.

When I got home the next afternoon from school, Mum said, "Dad wants you to go to Paris tonight. It's for hair and wardrobe fittings for *A Walk with Love and Death*."

"Oh, God," I said. "Do I have to?"

"I guess, darling, if you want to be an actress."

I changed into the yellow wool suit and left for Heathrow airport in a taxi. When I arrived in Paris, I was taken for costume fittings with the artist Leonor Fini at her atelier. I tried on a voluminous wig with clusters of gold braid at Alexandre de Paris's salon. He was Elizabeth Taylor's hairdresser. That day, student riots broke out on the Left Bank, and all the flights from Orly to London were canceled. Making every attempt to avoid my father, I was stranded for the next four days in my yellow wool suit, which had started to pill and stretch, without so much as a hairbrush or toothpaste in my possession. Finally, I took a taxi through the demonstration to get on a plane back to London.

The wheels were in motion for *A Walk with Love and Death*. The studio wanted still photographs, and the important British photographer Norman Parkinson was engaged at significant expense to do a sitting with me. I applied my usual mask of makeup, with additional eyelashes, pearly highlighter, and the sweep of black shadow in the crease of the eye. When Dad saw the stills, he was horrified and demanded that a session be set up with Eve Arnold.

Eve was a Magnum photographer who had worked on *The*

Misfits. We were sent off to some ruins in the Irish countryside with explicit instructions that my face be unsullied by so much as a speck of makeup. I felt unpleasantly exposed, but Eve was as kind as she could be and made no judgments. I grew to love her very much, and we worked together often throughout the years.

A Walk with Love and Death was at first postponed, and later the location was moved to Austria, as Paris was still in a state of unrest. Assaf Dayan, the son of the Israeli prime minister and war hero Moshe Dayan, was to play my love interest. But I had a crush on the boy who was playing my cousin in the film, Anthony Corlan. The three of us were taking off to the local funfair to ride go-karts in the evenings. I was distracted and having trouble learning my part, and avoiding Dad as much as possible in my off hours. During a scene where I was to describe the murder of my father, a nobleman (played by Dad, inciden-tally), I forgot my lines, and he lit into me in front of the crew with such ferocity that I hyperventilated. In another scene, I was to kiss Assaf, half-nude on a riverbank, and I did this two inches away from the nose of my angry, impatient father.

For the final fortnight of the shoot, we flew to Italy to do some exteriors. I was asked by the production department if I would go to the studio of the new set photographer to have my portrait taken for publicity stills for the movie. I was told to bring some personal clothes and jewelry. Midway through the session, I was surprised when he asked me to remove my top, and although it made me uncomfortable, I complied with his request. I had done several scenes in the film that required par-tial nudity, and assumed it was part of the assignment.

I was lonesome for Mum. Before I left for Austria, I'd met a new friend, an art student, at one of our dinner parties. He was a friend of Peter Menegas and his name was Jeremy Railton. We'd begun a romance before I left London, and he was now staying as a guest at Maida Avenue, in my room, under my Chinese bedspread. He wrote that he was having a good time with Mum. But then Tony wrote that Mum had not been in good form lately and that the atmosphere in London was "approaching the tragic." In his letter, he said he'd gone to her room a couple of days before to find her crying in her bed. She had claimed it was the weather, and he had put on a detached expression, because he did not want to engage in her personal problems, lest he get trapped.

Tony felt that her world must have crumbled as we became adults but that this was a fact of life, and to draw out the parting would make it all the more painful. He remarked that Mum was an exceptionally motherly woman; all her friends were children who needed looking after, which was one reason she had no older friends. But one old friend had returned to the scene—John Julius. It was a relationship that could hardly leave frivolity in its wake. Mum's efforts to seem gay and lighthearted around him reminded Tony of bad funny postcards. He said that lighthearted was not the way she felt and that Mum was no actress. Tony and I had begun to dread Mum's sadness, resenting that she confided her pain to her friends even as she isolated herself from us.

Tony offered to write to Dad on my behalf—since I found it hard to speak to him—or to speak to Dad with me in the room. He advised me that a concentrated study of literature was important, though achieving A-level exams was a little irrelevant if I was to be an actress. He pointed out that once I was able to judge a script's artistic merit, I would be able to make up my mind whether it was worth my time. He apologized for sounding pompous and offered to come over to Austria, should it be helpful. I don't think I ever acknowledged that letter. I felt that Mum had asked him to plea bargain with Dad for me.

Because I was under twenty-one when we filmed *A Walk with Love and Death,* my payment for the film was placed in a Swiss bank account. My father's lawyers had made it all but impossible for me to access my own money. But on the way back from Austria, I went to the tiny town of Chur, nestled high in the Swiss Alps, and withdrew enough money to pay for a platinum watch Mum had talked about having seen in the window of Cartier on Bond Street.

Returning to London, I found myself, by an amusing twist of fate, in a twelve-seat airplane flying with the Monkees. I was wearing a fetching yellow, embroidered Afghan jacket that smelled strongly of goat. On a whim, I decided to be French and took to answering their polite line of questioning with Gallic shrugs and broken English. As the journey progressed through the snowy night, Davy Jones invited me to their concert, and upon arrival at Heathrow, Davy and his manager offered to drop me off at my house in their limousine. When we came to Maida Avenue, they walked me to my door. Mum opened it. "Bonjour, Maman!" I exclaimed, and I introduced them to her in heavily accented English. As they wandered back to their car, I waved—"Bonsoir"—and shut the door.

"Now, what was all that about?" asked Mum.

I was in my bedroom one morning, soon after I came back from *A Walk with Love and Death,* when Mum walked in holding a copy of an Italian soft-porn magazine. I think it was called *Playman.* Inside was a photograph of me, nude to the waist, with a bemused expression on my face.

"I cannot imagine how this happened," said Mum. "Sometimes they use tricks, like putting your head on someone else's body, but I know what you look like without your clothes on."

I was embarrassed and ashamed and very worried about what Dad might do or say. But to his credit, he never spoke to me about the incident. Although I hate to think what happened to the photographer.

I wrapped the Cartier watch in its little red box in sheets and sheets of newspaper, so that Mum would think it was an enormous gift. It was almost worth all the problems I'd had on *A Walk with Love and Death*—a moment of great pride for me to be able to buy Mum something she desired.

A few months later I was asked by British *Vogue* to go to Paris to be photographed for the collections by David Bailey. I was flattered, and happily accepted. Upon arriving in Paris, I was surprised to learn that I would have a companion in the pictures, and I practically fell over when I learned that, ironically, it would be Willy Fox. All the next day, we worked for Bailey's camera, and all day I tried to be cool and keep my distance. That night after shooting, we went to Castel's, and there, lo and behold, was Arnaud de Rosnay. He and I danced and he said, "Come on, let's go somewhere!"

I said, "I'm going back to the Crillon. Call me upstairs in half an hour."

I returned to the hotel with the others, with Willy giving me the full press, determined to take me to his room. I pleaded fatigue and shut my door, and when Arnaud called a few minutes later, I ran downstairs and jumped into his Ferrari. We went to his aunt's deserted mansion in the Bois de Boulogne and made love on his big wolf coat by candlelight till dawn. By my loose standards at the time, a fine case of revenge.

Arnaud was a sweetheart. A gorgeous athlete, a real old-fashioned French playboy. He married one of James Gold-smith's beautiful daughters, Isabel, and invented a board game called Petropolis, which was like Monopoly but with gold-dipped oil rigs to replace hotels and houses. He presented one of these games to me, much later, when he came to visit California. He disappeared not long after, in 1984, windsurfing to Taiwan on the China Seas.

I had been studying for A-levels at a crammers, Davies Laing and Dick, when Mum took me to a party at the apartment of Tony Richardson. He was one of the important film directors of the time, making quintessentially new-wave British films like *A Taste of Honey, The Loneliness of the Long Distance Runner, Tom Jones,* and *The Charge of the Light Brigade.* He told me that he and his partner Neil Hartley were mounting a stage production of *Hamlet* starring Nicol Williamson, and he suggested that I might like to try out for the role of Ophelia. I subsequently read for Tony but did not get the part. It went to Marianne Faithfull, the girlfriend of Mick Jagger. From the moment I saw her, I found her astonishingly pretty. In the dark overhang of the Roundhouse, where the play was in rehearsal, it felt like the interior of a great ship, and sitting in a halo of light, in a pink angora dress and white tights, she was the baddest angel I'd ever seen. So, as it happened, I didn't mind at all when I got the chance to understudy her.

Built in 1847 on Chalk Farm Road to the north of Camden Town in North London, the Roundhouse had been conceived as a railway engine shed containing a turntable for the London and Birmingham Railway. It was a circular structure, gloomy and cavernous, that smelled of creosote, with enormous wooden beams. Within a decade, trains had become too large for the building and the Roundhouse was used for various purposes. In the mid-sixties it had become the scene for love-ins, rock concerts, happenings, and the like. With the addition of a proscenium stage rigged for lighting and the construction of a few dressing rooms, it began its new life as a theater.

Nicol Williamson, a tall, laconic Scottish actor, played the part of Hamlet with a nasal twang and a partial lisp; this was not an affectation but Nicol's natural speaking voice, and without doubt broke through some conceits as to how the Great Dane should be portrayed. Tony and Nicol rarely seemed to agree, and Tony munched nervously through a succession of green apples throughout the period of rehearsal. Anthony Hopkins was playing King Claudius and Judy Parfitt was Gertrude, and their chemistry was powerful. But after the show was up and running, Nicol would on occasion leave the stage without warning. This was always an interesting moment for the rest of the cast, who, without benefit of a curtain, would trail offstage after him into the wings in mute embarrassment. But Nicol was also an amazing actor and had a very strong presence; he was always entertaining to watch.

One night, the tip flew off his fencing foil in the graveyard scene and out into the audience. Nicol calmly stopped the action and asked if everyone was okay. Then crying, "On with the show!" he fell to the ground as Michael Pennington, playing Laertes, immediately stabbed him. Marianne Faithfull and I were both flirting with Nicol; we spent some time in his dressing room between shows. One evening at dinner after a performance, he introduced me to his friend Ian Holm, an idol of mine since I had seen his ground-breaking performance as Richard III at the National Theatre.

Marianne often would ease into the dressing room so close to curtain that I was already wearing her costume. I'd whip it off and start to lace her up in it as she'd pin the waist-length blond wig to her hair and then wander onstage in a cloud of Robert Piguet's Fracas perfume, a heavy distillation of hypnotic tuberose.

One night Mum gave a party for the American artist Kenneth Nolan; he came with the art critic Clement Greenberg and a pretty brunette girlfriend called Stephanie Gordon, in a blue Pucci minidress. The next day, I heard Mum and Gina Medcalf talking about how the guests had been smoking grass. A girl called Jenny Harrington, with red hair and sweet green eyes, came one night. She was only nineteen, closer to my age than Mum's, and another Sunday she in turn brought two of her friends, a black actor called Stefan Kalifa and his friend Brian Henderson, a handsome young musician from Trinidad. They took Mum and me to a club in Paddington, where there was a reggae group called the Heptones, who sang a song that I loved called "I Need a Fat Girl," aka "Fatty Fatty."

I'm in the mood, the mood
I need a fat, fat girl tonight

Soon Mum was seeing more of Brian.

CHAPTER 13

Anjelica and Ricki running along
Maida Avenue, 1968

Mum was planning to drive to Venice to see her friend Manina, and while she'd spoken with me about it, she hadn't told me that she was going with anyone. We hadn't seen John Julius for some time, and I suspected that she was going with Brian. Allegra was to stay behind with Nurse. The night before she was to leave, she came into my room under the pretext of wanting to borrow one of my weekly women's magazines. She sat on my bed. Eventually, she just got around to it and said, "You know, Anjel, we need to talk, because things are changing very fast. You're becoming a woman, and you're going to want to see boys and have lovers. We've been living in an atmosphere of secrecy lately. I feel it in you, and you feel it in me. But we're together in the same house, and we're mother and daughter. It's difficult, but we're going to have to incorporate it into our lives, because it's a factor now. Unless you're going to go and live somewhere else, which maybe you'd like to consider. This is an issue we're going to have to face."

I burst into tears. We sat on the Chinese bedspread, and we hugged and cried. It seemed possible that everything could become honest between us again. For a whole year I had come home from pretending to be at school and she'd be crying in her bed. I had become secretive and devious. Mum was obviously very upset about the failed relationship with John Julius and the wall of silence that had divided us. She stood up and went into her room. And I was flooded with love for her.

The morning after our conversation, I was sitting at the piano downstairs in the living room, tapping the keys, as Mum was preparing to leave. She had asked me for some tapes to take on her trip, and I'd picked out some music for her—Miles Davis, Dylan, the Stones, Vivaldi's *The Four Seasons*. She seemed in a rush to go, which tipped me off that she would have company. She was wearing makeup and looked very pretty. We hugged and I told her to have a good time. The front door closed behind her and the house was silent. I went to rehearsals at the Roundhouse. A few days later, Nurse said, "I haven't heard from Madam." That was strange and it worried us, since Mum used to call every day to ask about Allegra, who was only four at the time.

I had a dream that night that my spine was being pulled out

of me. I heard a voice saying, "Wake up, Anjelica. Wake up."
I opened my eyes. Leslie Waddington was sitting on my bed.
I thought, *What the hell is Leslie Waddington doing sitting on my
bed?* Then he said, "Your mother's dead. She was killed in a car
crash." I felt my heart imploding while my mind tried to grasp
what he had said.

When I walked downstairs, I saw that the house had changed
overnight. I think Allegra was upstairs napping. The unthinkable had happened. Nurse was weeping. I couldn't bear to look
to her or Tony for confirmation. The light had gone out of
everything. It was like being in a pile of ashes. Tony and I were
silent. What could we say? We didn't hug or touch.

Leslie said, "We should tell Allegra in Ricki's room." So we
went upstairs to Mum's room, and we sat on her bed. I sat on
the right, and Tony sat on the left, with Allegra between us and
Nurse opposite. Leslie told Allegra that her mummy had gone
away and wouldn't be coming back. Allegra opened her mouth
and let out a scream like a banshee. A terrible, sad, high-pitched
scream. An awful sound. Like something being torn out of your
guts. Then Nurse took her to her room. Later that afternoon,
she was reading aloud from her bird book.

I went into Mum's closet. Her dresses didn't even smell like
her anymore. Flowers were coming. Lots of flowers; violets
from Dick Avedon, violets from Diana Cooper. I was furious
at the flowers. What the hell? Flowers can't replace my mum.

I took a taxi to the Roundhouse and sat in the empty theater.
In a way, I looked forward to the drama of telling Tony Richardson. When he walked in with Neil Hartley, I said it quick,
"Mum's dead," and I watched the horror spread across their
faces. That was really my proof that it had even happened—the
effect of the news on other people. That evening Tony and I

had to go to Victoria Station to meet Dad, who was coming in from Rome. He had been diagnosed with emphysema, and his lungs were so bad he couldn't fly. When he got off the train, he looked terrible. Gaunt and white-faced. We must have gone to Claridge's with him, always his hotel of choice. Other than the initial greeting on the station platform, I don't recall a single embrace or any word of consolation. But then he might have known that I blamed him for abandoning her.

Later, at 31 Maida Avenue, Willy Fox came to the door in a tan raincoat, walked in, and came upstairs. He lay outside the covers and held me until I fell asleep. I'll never forget him for that.

Mum's funeral was on February 8, 1969. The house began to fill up with people, Mum's friends, my friends. It was as if shock had made time stand still. Joan flew in from New York to take care of me; she remembers the iron four-poster bed at the end of the garden, covered with snow.

Manina wrote to me from Venice:

> *It is impossible—still—for me to conceive it. I just cannot imagine a world without Ricki. She is one of the lights of my life, and will remain so. I see her magnified and magic. When she appeared she changed everything; life became a feast. As if everything was suddenly possible. She was a container of life itself. Maybe so much that there remained nothing to live for anymore.*

At Mum's funeral, Jules Buck came up to Dad with his palm extended. He wanted to make peace, but Dad turned his back on him. He never spoke to Jules again. There was no casket in the crowded room at the Friends meetinghouse. My mother always said that the one religion she truly respected was Quakerism. I remember nothing of the service or what anyone said.

From Gladys Hill to Dorothy Jeakins:

> 23 Three Kings Yard
> London W1, England
> Feb. 11, 1969

Dorothy darling—

I received your dear letter and will ask Anjelica and Tony about a memento of Ricki's for you.

She was on her way to Lago Maggiore with a young jazz musician named Brian Thomas Henderson. He was driving. We have not seen the police report yet but, near Dijon, near a small town called Gray, in Eastern France, they collided with a truck. It was Ricki's car. She was killed instantly and Henderson was cut about the face, concussed. Henderson is still in hospital there. The truck driver was injured in the leg. But both men will recover nicely. The Memorial Service was held Saturday in the Westminster Meeting Hall, Society of Friends. The Quaker elders conducted the service and it was a half hour of silence with the elders speaking occasionally—words of comfort and simple faith! It was a miraculous service of rare beauty and dignity. I shall tell you about it when next we meet.

There was no will and I am trying to help with inventory and that kind of thing.

John and Tony go on to Ireland tonight. Anjelica is understudying Ophelia in Tony Richardson's "Hamlet" that opens here Feb. 17th. Nurse and Allegra are at the house and Gina Medcalf, a young friend of Ricki's, is sleeping there. Little by little, all will be straightened out. Anjelica and Tony are doing well—and so is John. Also Allegra and Nurse.

Leslie Waddington took over for all the hard things—what an exceptional young man he is!

Betty was here until yesterday. I shall be on my own here tomorrow.

I am sending this to Santa Barbara because you will have finished in Guaymas. And will write more later.

Much love from all of us,
Gladys xxxxxxs

That line, so stoic, so fiercely optimistic: "Both men will recover nicely"! I don't know about the truck driver, but I believe my mother's death haunted Brian Henderson throughout his life.

Marianne was kind to me. She took me along when she went to buy drugs at Boots Pharmacy in Piccadilly in her chauffeur-driven Bentley. Once we went to see a doctor friend of hers who chased us around his surgery, an action both disturbing and funny. But we got out of there in a hurry, and Marianne took me to her house on Cheyne Walk, opened a door upstairs, and showed me her infant son, sleeping in his crib. Mick Jagger came home later that evening. I thought he was amazing—rail thin, with sexy, insolent eyes and full lips. Having admired him as a schoolgirl, I found meeting him in person quite surreal.

Marianne gave me her long red fox coat and kissed me goodbye. She was off to Australia with Mick to do the film *Ned Kelly*. I had hoped again that Tony would allow me to play the part, but Francesca Annis took over the role of Ophelia before *Hamlet* went on tour to New York. Even though I had only a walk-on appearance in the play as a lady-in-waiting, I saw the trip to New York as an opportunity to escape the terrible emptiness of Maida Avenue. I didn't know what Dad might have in store for me.

On March 1, a little over a month after Mum died, Gladys wrote from the Palace Hotel in Helsinki, telling me that before she put Mum's good jewelry and lesser costume pieces into storage, she wanted to pass on a piece of polished stone, a medallion, to Dorothy Jeakins. She told me that my mother had rings and her pearl necklace from my father with her in Gray, and closed the letter by saying, "I have had no word on Mr. Henderson, but am sure that when he returns to England, he will want to talk to you, which is right. But see him only the once, for you and he could never be friends, and your good taste and natural dignity will tell you this."

I received a call from Brian, who told me he had some things he wanted to give to me. When I went to his flat, he presented me with a dream that Mum had written down the night before the accident and some things she had with her when she died. He returned the Cartier watch that I'd given to her for her birthday; the oval glass had shattered over the Roman numerals. And he gave me the box of music I'd sent her off with on her journey. He obviously hadn't looked inside. I took the box home and went into my bathroom and locked the door. When I opened it, the tapes fell out covered in dark, sticky blood. In shock, I dropped them in the bathtub, turned on the tap, and watched the water run red on the porcelain and down the drain. Later that night, I read the dream.

JAN 28–29

ST. QUENTIN GRAND HOTEL

I am in a room with B. Perhaps in bed.
There is a stillness. There will be an earthquake.
The hotel crumbles. There is wreckage everywhere.

We have slipped gently to a place somewhere
atop it. I can see colored shreds and strips
of building refuse that is neither wood nor steel
but something like both. There is no feeling of
danger but of something like relief—that
sort of calm after a storm.

Lucio wrote to tell me he had photographs "of many of her expressions, whether épanouic or with melancholy—she was like that—extremist." He said she improved many things within him, and that she had helped him at a certain moment of his life.

Tony and I separated Mum's collection of photographs from her diaries and letters. I kept the former, and Tony stored her papers in a trunk. Later, when Allegra retrieved the trunk, she read what was there. One discovery was that Mum had terminated a pregnancy in 1959, the year she broke up with Lucio García del Solar.

Philippe Halsman, who had taken my mother's photograph so long before for the cover of *Life,* wrote that he felt he had been instrumental in changing the course of her life from an ordinary to an extraordinary one, and was asking himself whether it had been for her ultimate good.

Joan wrote that she was delighted I was coming to New York that spring, and sent me a beautiful letter:

Please don't cry; we shall laugh as much as your mother and
I did when she came to this heathen land, for you and she have
the same mind and the same humor, the same way of looking at
the world and knowing that it's a bit off. I saw Arnaud who was
white through his tan at the news and says he really loves you: the

192

town is sad and grey but it will be sort of beige by the time you get here.

I used to say, "Oh, will you leave me that in your will?" when I liked jewels or dresses or something of Mum's. It was a joke, of course. It never occurred to me that my mother would die young. My father, it was one thing, he could've gone at any minute, and all anyone did was talk about my father's health. But my mother—it was different; she was only thirty-nine.

I think of my mother all the time. Diana Pickersgill's mother, Dorothy, died in a car crash, too. Diana described such a loss as an abduction, and so it is.

PART THREE

NEW YORK

Avedon for *Vogue*, 1972

CHAPTER 14

Anjelica in Connemara, the west
of Ireland, for *Vogue,* 1969

On April 28, 1969, I went to live with Joan on Forty-seventh Street at the Buchanan, in an apartment belonging to her uncle Don. It was around the corner from the Shelton Hotel on Lexington Avenue, home away from the skies for a stream of uniformed pilots and female flight attendants who seemed to be having a good time of it. Downstairs, Smiler's deli made fat tuna-salad sandwiches on rye, and Schrafft's across the street mixed a great chocolate ice cream soda. Joan took me to Serendipity and made me buy an elegant black jumpsuit. We were happy as roommates; she allowed me to paint my room a lurid magenta, which was a mistake. I went on to decorate her living room in an Indonesian jungle theme with a bamboo overhang entwined with green rubber snakes and inflatable lizards.

Joan was running with a crowd of photographers, designers, illustrators, editors, and models; she seemed to prefer the company of French people. Soon she would be making plans to go to Paris to work as a stylist for the photographer Guy Bourdin, whose brilliant and surreal work at French *Vogue* was causing a sensation. She introduced me to his assistant, a doll-faced Vietnamese called Duc, with whom I began a rather tranquil liaison. He spoke little French and barely a word of English.

Joan spent many of her nights encased in a see-through plastic hazmat suit in order to make her ankles thin. She was now an assistant fashion editor at *Glamour* and was writing book reviews for the magazine. She was finally exercising her talent and her interests. She was working with the top photographers and spoke knowledgeably about Richard Avedon, Hiro, Bert Stern, Irving Penn, and an emerging group of more radical photographers whose pictures were having a major impact on fashion—names like Helmut Newton, Jimmy Moore, and Bob Richardson.

She showed me a copy of French *Vogue*. Among the photographs on the fashion pages, Bob Richardson's work was singular. The model, Donna Mitchell, was intense. In several of the pictures, she looked beautiful but distraught. In others, she was wearing Moroccan harem pants, talismans, and Hindi tattoos, stranded on a Greek beach with a naked lover washing up against the rocks of a tide pool. Looking at this layout was like watching a beautiful, dangerous foreign movie. It was not about fashion. Joan said to me, "If you want to be a model, you should really work with Richardson."

In those first weeks in New York, I would walk back to the apartment after the curtain at the Lunt-Fontanne, where we were doing *Hamlet.* Now that Francesca Annis had taken over for Marianne, I never got to go on as understudy. I zigzagged through the neon-stained streets at night with the tall glass buildings towering around me and steam percolating from the manholes, passing the cheap radio-and-discount-camera stores on Broadway, the bodegas, the joke-and-souvenir shops with latex masks of Richard Nixon and Spiro Agnew next to small replicas of Marilyn Monroe and the Statue of Liberty. I had a love-hate relationship with the city from the start. New York ran all the extremes. She was the beast that didn't sleep, where you could find whatever you were looking for in twenty minutes. As often as not, along Sixth Avenue, I would pass the solitary blind Viking, "Moondog," in his red tunic under a helmet of giant Valkyrie horns, and he would recite a poem. A magical, iconic denizen of the city, he was like something ancient from outer space.

A few times, after hours, Joan took me down to Max's Kansas City on Park Avenue South. Initially, it was hard to comprehend her enthusiasm for this funky nightclub and diner in a grim part of town, with its red-and-black interior, chickpeas on the tables, and a clientele who seemed to consist of drug addicts, crazies, hookers, artists, models, poets, and transvestites. But there was a seedy attraction to the place. It was there that I came to meet some of the many dark souls, wayward spirits, and lost children of New York. It was a moment when angst and irony came together and little was sacred.

When I think of the faces, it is always by artificial light. Andy Warhol at his customary table, like the white rabbit of Alice's tea party, surrounded by his transsexual sirens: Candy Darling, Holly Woodlawn, Jackie Curtis, and Ondine. The actor Michael Pollard, fresh from the screen in *Bonnie and Clyde,* was often there, as was his friend the musician Bobby Neuwirth, the brilliant illustrator Antonio Lopez, the bombshell Amanda Lear, and the actress Sylvia Miles, a graying blond with a thick Bronx accent and chipped nail polish, dripping in black jet beads, torn lace, and old velvet—all these people clinging to their nocturnal perches above Union Square.

Once in a while I'd go to Grandpa's restaurant for lunch, and he would sit me down in a red leather banquette and order steak and spinach for me. He told me that I would never be as beautiful as my mother but that I had character and it would serve me well. He was consumed with sadness over Mum's death and blamed Dad, who he declared was a gambler.

I got a call from an editor at *Harper's Bazaar* who said they wanted to take my picture for the magazine. I guess it was early publicity for *A Walk with Love and Death.* They had chosen Bob Richardson as the photographer. A few days later, Bob showed up at the Lunt-Fontanne stage door in a tiny little open-roofed red Fiat. A big blond poodle sat in the backseat. It was an arresting sight. Bob introduced himself and the dog: "This is Lucky."

Bob was tall and rangy, very thin, with high cheekbones, a strong chin, and knowing, empathetic gray eyes. His teeth jutted in an overbite, which made his lips pout, and he was self-conscious when he smiled. He had curly gray hair and wore a white shirt, blue jeans, and a black fedora with a straight brim. He drove us out of New York past the smokestacks and the refineries to a stretch of sand, Jones Beach, forty-five minutes from the city.

Awaiting us was the fashion editor, who, as I recall, dressed me in a long skirt and a peasant blouse with a red velvet waist-coat. Bob and I walked up into the dunes overlooking the water; the wind rustled through the sea grass. Bob told me he had been working on a back-to-nature series; he said it was the wave of the future. He held a Nikon delicately in his long slender hands and studied me for a while. When it started to feel dangerous, he'd lift the camera to his eye and take the picture. He stared at me so penetratingly, I felt that he could follow the ebb and flow of my emotions. He lowered the camera and looked deeply into my eyes. He'd shot only a couple of reels. "We have the picture," he said.

Bob had grown up on Long Island, one of six children in an Irish Catholic family. During high school, he made thousands of line drawings and paintings—"cars and airplanes, bottles and boxes, clothes and accessories"—and began drawing women. After graduating, he enrolled at Parsons School of Design and then Pratt Institute in Brooklyn for graphic design.

In the forties, a friend gave Bob a Rolleiflex camera. He shot a still life and never painted a landscape again. He said once that he always photographed loneliness, because that was his life, and the pictures were about himself. In the fifties, Bob married for the first time and fought in Korea. When he returned to America, he learned that his wife, Barbara, was an alcoholic. He claimed she was hostile and jealous, and they divorced.

In the sixties, Bob was discovered by *Harper's Bazaar* editors

Marvin Israel and Diana Vreeland and began to shoot for the magazine. He said that his photographs were often deemed "too dark, too real, and too sexual for publication," but he was also erratic, and that scared a lot of people. Danger fascinated Bob; he was more of a reporter than a fashion photographer.

In 1963, Bob married his second wife, Norma, a Copacabana dancer who went on to work with him as a fashion stylist. Two years later, they had a son, Terry. The family moved to Paris and lived for a couple of years in the 16th arrondissement. When they returned to New York in the late sixties, they took an apartment on Jane Street in the Village. It was soon after this that I met Bob, when he received the call asking if he wanted to photograph me for *Harper's Bazaar.*

I don't remember what happened immediately following my first encounter with Bob Richardson, or when he told me that he and Norma were separating, or how he convinced me so quickly that we belonged together. But I felt that he could see into my soul almost in a psychic way, like Mum. And I believed that he would be my champion and teacher and protector. He wrote short, passionate notes to me: "I will spend my time loving you." "You will never be alone." "You will always be with the man who loves you." "Each year you will grow more beautiful, and I shall love you more each year."

The first time we made love, Bob placed me in front of a mirror and we smoked a joint together. It was almost an out-of-body experience. I felt we were the same animal, the same breed, although he was much older than I. Bob was forty-two; I had just turned eighteen.

In the early summer, when I was on tour in Boston with *Hamlet,* Bob came to visit. There was a brass four-poster bed in my hotel room, and he played the tape of Dylan's *Nashville Skyline* album, with the song "Lay Lady Lay." I felt a sense of destiny in being with him.

When the run in Boston ended, *Hamlet* toured to Chicago. I didn't want to remain with the company and decided to return to New York. Bob insisted that I stay with him at the Gramercy Park Hotel. He had a studio downtown on Fifth Avenue, and often, after he left the hotel for work, I would spend the mornings watching soap operas—*As the World Turns* and *Days of Our Lives*—interspersed with bulletins about thousands of people in Washington marching against the Vietnam War and attacks on protesters by construction workers referred to in the news as "hard-hats."

Working with Dad had not been an experience I longed to duplicate, so I decided to give acting a rest. Fortunately, at just that moment Dick Avedon called to ask if I would let him photograph me for *Vogue.* I was very excited at the prospect of working with Dick, having entertained dreams of high fashion since before I posed for him in London, when he declared to Mum that my shoulders were "too broad."

Dick Avedon was the most famous fashion photographer in the world. His studio was the Holy Grail for a model—what every girl dreamed of. He'd loved my mother and always had a soft spot for me. Avedon was legendary for making women look beautiful, and he had photographed the most beautiful women in the world—from Dovima at the circus, among the elephants in Dior couture, to Suzy Parker, running from the paparazzi at the Place Vendôme in Paris, to Verushka, Jean Shrimpton, and Lauren Hutton, leaping like exotic birds in midflight across the pages of *Vogue.* Avedon himself was the model for the role of the photographer played by Fred Astaire in *Funny Face.*

When I think of Dick, most often he is standing alert beside his tripod-mounted Hasselblad camera, his face close to the lens, a line to the shutter between his thumb and index finger. He wears a crisp white shirt, Levi's, and moccasins. His black-framed glasses travel from the bridge of his nose up to his forehead. As he focuses, he sweeps back a forelock of thick gray hair when it falls across his eyes. His gaze is keen and critical. He understands glamour like no other photographer. Dick's studio exuded an atmosphere of luxury and taste, a place where art and industry dovetailed harmoniously. Although I considered him a friend first, I rarely saw him socially. He was one of the grown-ups.

Polly Mellen was the fashion editor with whom Avedon worked most at *Vogue,* under the grand and exotic reign of "the Empress," Diana Vreeland. Polly was emotional and intense, with the profile of an Indian brave, under a short, straight, steel-gray bob. Before a sitting, Polly's assistants would arrange racks of shoes, bags, accessories, and jewelry on long refectory tables. Working for *Vogue* was a big production, and the studio assistants were constantly on the move, urgently following directions.

I sensed the challenge to come up to par, all of us seeking out the excitement of that moment when the elements came together and a picture got made. There was a rush like no other when Dick called out smoothly, "Beautiful," above the music, and Polly's eyes shone with pride, and the rhythm of the shutter accelerated along with the white flash of the strobe light. Sometimes I'd be shaking when I walked off the no-seam paper, returning to the dressing room.

Diana Vreeland had taken a liking to me, and consequently assigned Dick, the fashion editor Babs Simpson, and Ara Gallant, who did fascinating and unexpected things with hair, to work on what would become a twenty-eight-page feature in Ireland. I was called up to Ms. Vreeland's office at the top of the Graybar Building. The corridors were monochromatic beige and lined with workspaces occupied by cool, efficient women. Cutouts from magazines, photographs, and swatches of fabric were pinned to the walls of the cubicles. The low hum of fashion's tension built the closer one came to Ms. Vreeland's lair.

As I recall, the interior of her office was lipstick red, and the carpet was leopard-skin print. On the wall to the right was a collage of exquisite images, including the head of Marlon Brando and the foot of Rudolf Nureyev. The woman herself was tall and imperious, with a large nose and a helmet of jet-black hair back-combed into the shape and texture of a stag beetle. Her cheeks were rosy and her mouth a full, deep crimson. Her small dark eyes glittered pointedly at me as she indicated the racks of clothes that had been selected. An hour or so into trying on outfits, I fainted dead away and came to with Ms. Vreeland gently slapping my cheeks and barking for an editor to bring me water.

Bob was unhappy with my plan to go to Ireland and voiced his concern that I would not be coming back. I did my best to assure him that I would return. However, I couldn't refuse this great opportunity to travel with Avedon. I was beginning to get comfortable in my own skin, and I enjoyed working for the camera. Dick had decided that he wanted the story to be about a couple traveling in the West Country in a painted tinker caravan, and in an effort to include me, he'd shown me pictures of beautiful young men as potential photographic partners. I rejected an image of the singer-songwriter James Taylor and chose as my companion an attractive blond, Harvey Mattison.

On July 11, 1969, we arrived in Ireland. We were staying

at a small hotel out in the Connemara wilderness when the astronauts landed on the moon for the first time. Looking up at the moon's sad white face, her mouth a shadowy crater, I felt intensely protective of her, as if her purity had been invaded.

Ara Gallant and I became fast friends. We laughed because we were in Ireland and Ara abhorred the color green. I always thought Ara just appeared one day on earth. He was diminutive in stature but moved like a flamenco dancer in his high-heeled cowboy boots. Gay, of Russian-Jewish origin, and a full-blown New Yorker, Ara wore black at all times, a sailor's pigtail to his waist, with chiseled sideburns ending in a point beneath his cheekbones, and a Kangol spitfire hat full of charms on top of his dark curls.

Once we were out on the bogs, Ara and I teased Harvey mercilessly. I asked him to dive into a freezing lake to capture a water lily. He was very brave, but he almost got hypothermia.

Dick had expressed a desire to take my picture with a falcon on my arm, and as a result we found ourselves at a private avian sanctuary at the home of a German baron in Co. Meath. We were astonished to see his commendations from the German army hanging behind glass in a cabinet inside the front door. When he came downstairs to greet us, the baron was wearing spats, jodhpurs, a stock, and a monocle. He was actually flexing a little whip. Dick almost fainted.

We were escorted outside by several efficient workmen and shown the baron's amazing collection of fierce birds: owls and hawks of various species, several of which were placed on my fist for Dick to photograph. All in all, it was a very strange scene, with the baron barking in German to the bird handlers, and the talons of the raptors digging into my wrist. We were not unhappy to leave the baron's estate.

Our little caravan traveled from Dublin to Tipperary to Limerick to Galway. Dick photographed us in the fields and the bogs, romping in haystacks, running through gorse, and playing in ruined castles. When we were in Dingle, Dick made the mistake of handing out a few shillings to a bunch of tinker children from the window of our car. The next thing, they were clinging to the windshield and the bumper, jumping and banging on the roof. In those days, there was an enormous amount of poverty in rural Ireland. Eventually, Dick, Ara, Harvey, and Babs left for New York after dropping me off at St. Clerans.

Allegra and Nurse were now in residence at the Little House. Leslie Waddington had offered to raise Allegra after Mum died, but it became evident that it was too much for him and his new wife to take on this small, autocratic little girl, as well as Nurse, who was devastated by Mum's death.

Allegra's father, John Julius, was married with two children. Later he said that after Mum died, his wife, Anne, offered to raise Allegra alongside her teenage brother and sister, but Dad had intervened and offered to bring her to Ireland. They reached an agreement that Dad would raise Allegra as his own daughter and John Julius "would be hitherto presented as her godfather." Recently, Allegra said, "John Julius could be accurately referred to as my father, but I had only one dad." I was proud of Dad when he agreed to raise Allegra at St. Clerans. It was a moving, openhearted gesture, and he loved her as his own, taking great pleasure in her intelligence and aptitude for learning. Finally I felt she was safe.

Later that summer, some six months after Mum's death, Allegra and Nurse came to Ireland. My little brother, Danny, was there with Zoë, his mother, so Danny and Allegra developed an early closeness. From St. Clerans I wrote to Joan in New York:

> *Generally it feels like an ex-orgy. Danny is fat and Italian and not too pretty, and I don't understand anything he says. Nevertheless, he appears quite likable, as he holds Allegra's hand and smiles a lot. Nurse is mixing and rapping with Mrs. Creagh, and happy as hell. It's beautiful to see them both here.*

Allegra was staying in my old bedroom at the Little House but didn't realize that everything there once was mine: the toys, the Japanese dolls, the music box, the books.

Dad was also due to come home. I was dreading the meeting that would take place between Bob and my father, and I did not invite Bob to come to Ireland. My instinct was that Dad would loathe him. It seemed inevitable. Bob had demanded that I meet up with him in London or we would "never see each other again." I booked the flight, but later that evening a telegram came, *Flight to London canceled, arrive in Paris Tuesday, your friend Bob Richardson.* Is he my *friend,* too? I wondered.

I wrote to Joan:

> *The Richardson tells me that he has seen much of you. He has also just about closed his little space-capsule about himself. First, I was leaving, getting into the big black limousine off to Ireland and it's all "I love you," and happily heartbreaking, and I am gone. And while I am gone, mysterious change. The conversations on the telephone start off "I love you," repeat, "I miss you," repeat. Then suddenly, the mood changes in front of my ears—*
>
> *"You've got to make up your mind."*

"What do you want?"
"You're trying to do me in."

I was worried about meeting Bob in Paris, because if things did not work out between us, I didn't dare think of the consequences. I had mistaken Bob's need for dominance and control as love. Nevertheless, I joined him at the Hotel Raphael in Paris, and we went on vacation to Marrakech. He bought me an exquisite white silk wedding hammock and a heavy black djellaba that made me look like a female Rasputin.

A Walk with Love and Death had opened poorly that fall, and I personally received some breathtakingly negative reviews. The film critic John Simon said, "There is a perfectly blank, supremely inept performance by Huston's daughter, Anjelica, who has the face of an exhausted gnu, the voice of an unstrung tennis racket, and a figure of no discernible shape."

I was not particularly thrilled to hear that Dad's publicist, Ernie Anderson, was organizing a schedule of appearances and talk shows to promote the film for Fox. There was a visit to an army barracks in Cleveland built into the schedule. I vaguely remember watching the K9s attacking a man in burlap. There were some stopovers in Boston and Chicago. My co-star, Assaf Dayan, was in from Tel Aviv, and we were booked to stay at the Plaza Hotel for the end of the junket. Bob had insisted that when I returned to New York, I should stay with him at the Gramercy Park, his hotel of choice. I did not want to disappoint Bob, so I explained the importance of switching hotels to Ernie, who kindly accommodated my request.

I was at the hotel having a bath when Bob walked in. We were so happy to see each other. We smoked some pot, ordered up a slice of pecan pie and another of cheesecake, made love, and went to sleep. I had a wake-up call for early in the morning, as I was to appear for a taping of the *Tonight* show. When the phone rang, Bob did not stir. It was still dark when I tiptoed out, careful not to wake him. I had not yet unpacked but had pulled out of my suitcase the white satin shirt and python maxi skirt and vest I'd had made up at Carnaby Street in London, after my return from the *Walk with Love and Death* set in Austria. The *Tonight* show, one of the first on-air interviews I'd ever done, was unremarkable except for Johnny Carson's evident boredom. As I was answering a question, he'd invariably check his notebook for the next one. It was an odd style, quite unbalancing.

I was looking forward to getting back to the hotel room to see Bob. I turned the key quietly in the lock. By now it was mid-morning. When I opened the door, a single ray of light seeped through the join in the curtains, and I beheld a strange sight. Naked, like a martyr fallen from his cross, an arm flung across his eyes, his limbs so scattered as to look broken, Bob lay on a couch across the room. For a second, I wondered if he'd been attacked or mugged, but this was evidently not so. My torn dresses and broken jewelry littered the floor. Some garments clung to the window ledge, while others had made the journey through the open window to the pavement below, never to be recovered.

"What have I done?" I cried, casting off my stiff python suit and standing before him half naked. "Tell me, what have I done?" I cried again. I think this was an attempt to prove to him that I was unarmed, that I was not a threat. I stayed for hours with Bob in the darkened room, pleading with him to forgive me for leaving my suitcases unpacked. That had been my offense. In that short time, I had become the enemy.

I felt responsible for having hurt his feelings and was addled and shaken by his behavior. Even though I couldn't understand the train of thought that brought him to this state of confusion and despair, it was evident that he really cared a lot about me. Bob had a magic knack of knowing with great precision what was to be my breaking point, when he would become human and loving again. He said that because I had not unpacked my bags, it had made him feel temporary, unimportant, and insecure—this reaction should show me how much he loved me.

In the weeks that followed, there were other interviews, appearances, and obligations to the movie. By now Ernie had apprised Dad of my decision to stay in an alternative hotel with a boyfriend, and I had received a stern call from Dad saying that he did not like the sound of this arrangement and would be coming to New York imminently to check it out. I had nightmares of his showing up in the slightly shabby confines of the Gramercy Park Hotel lobby, ready to haul me off in chains to a nunnery. I burrowed down with Bob. Ernie Anderson called to tell me I was booked on *The David Frost Show*. The night before I was due to go on, I wept, telling Bob how much I missed Mum. "I'm scared of Dad," I told him. "He frightens me."

Bob exploded. "What are you saying? He's your father! He's the one you really love, the one you love the most! You know you love your father more than you ever loved your mother!"

He told me to apologize to my father on television for having been insensitive and difficult to work with, and for having disappointed him when he had done so much to help me. In fear and shock, I went out like a robot and did *The David Frost Show*. I said word for word what Bob had told me to say. After I got off the show, Ernie said, "Well, that should bring them in, if nothing else does!" David Frost named me as one of his most interesting interviews that year. I guess he hadn't interviewed Richard Nixon yet.

The truth was that I was confused and out of my depth while hopelessly attempting to make Bob happy. I was unaware of the extent and seriousness of his condition. I did not know that he was clinically sick, and I felt responsible for his pain. Anything, even the smallest thing, could threaten him or put him in a tailspin. It took several days for Bob to recover from these episodes, sometimes longer. He never told me that he used to hear voices and hallucinate badly. That he once destroyed his studio and was sent to a private clinic, where they placed him in a padded cell and put him in a straitjacket. Or that he had a brother who was diagnosed with paranoid schizophrenia. In time I learned that Bob was bipolar, schizophrenic, and bisexual. He had attempted suicide at twenty-two and at least four times in the years that followed, the evidence of which crisscrossed his veins in razor scars, from the wrists to the upper arms. I thought of Bob as a wounded soul and believed it was my mission to save him. When he would turn his head away from the wall and back to me, it was cause for celebration. We'd go around the corner to Luchow's and make up over a bottle of Lancer's rosé, and everything would look brighter.

Norma was now living in Woodstock with their four-year-old son, Terry, so on weekends Bob and I would often take the bus to Woodstock from the Port Authority on Forty-second Street, a derelict and ugly place, and watch out the window as the shabbiness of midtown Manhattan gave way to the green of the country. I loved Woodstock, with its rivers warm enough to wallow in during the summer. There was always something going on. Because it was a frontier town in music, they were all living there, from Richie Havens to Robbie Robertson and the Band to Bob Dylan. But if you wanted, you could just be quiet and cook and hang out, which was what I loved to do, and it gave Bob a chance to visit Terry.

Sometimes we would stay in a sort of open-house arrangement with a music-producer friend of Bob's, Ron Merian, and his wife, Valma. There was a story going around at the time about a very young, very pretty model of the moment who, one day, while tripping on LSD, jumped off a tree, thinking she could fly. She hit the ground and died. Although drugs were ubiquitous and always available, especially in a town like Woodstock, I was not tempted to try anything stronger than grass. The word "acid" scared me, and still does. When Bob and I heard that thousands of hippies were headed to Woodstock on August 15, 1969, we decided to stay in New York City, thereby missing out on a huge chunk of history.

CHAPTER 15

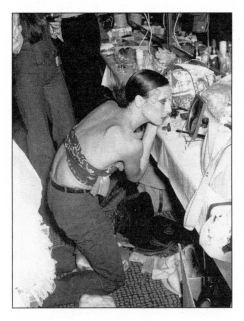

Anjelica applying makeup backstage
at Zandra Rhodes's charity fashion
show, London, 1973

Though the photographs from my trip to Ireland with Dick
Avedon had not yet run in *Vogue,* I had gained confidence
from the experience and had made up my mind that I wanted
to be a fashion model. I had always doubted my own physical
appeal but, oddly, I felt powerful in front of the camera.

215

When I told Bob that I wanted to be a model, he didn't laugh at me. He asked why I didn't want to act anymore. I told him that it was too painful, that the criticism was unbearable, and that I had lost my nerve. Bob said it was obvious that I needed to join an agency. He called Eileen Ford and asked if she would see me as a favor to him. I walked into Ford Models some few days later and was shown into Eileen's private suite. When I entered the room, a pert, freckled woman in her forties with a reddish bob and a girlish headband looked me smartly up and down. "Let's see your legs," she said.

I told her my ambition was to be photographed by Guy Bourdin, and she replied nastily, "What do you want, dearie? A plane ticket to Paris?" I ran home to Bob. Kindly, he consoled me. "We'll show her," he said. "She's just a pain in the ass." He assured me that Eileen had nothing against me, even though she was friends with his wife, Norma. Despite her testiness, she did take me on as a Ford model.

I was very shy and I loathed go-sees—walking through the streets of New York brandishing my two-foot-square modeling book full of photographs like a weapon, riding up in strange elevators to photography studios, mostly on the Lower East Side or downtown on Broadway, to be looked over like horseflesh. You never knew what might come out of the shadows. On one of my first meetings, a photographer leafed through the book and suggested we do some test shots. When I raised my arms in a pose, he exclaimed, "Don't fly away!" I ran to his desk and grabbed the book before darting down the emergency exit stairs in tears.

Again I confided in Bob. "Watch me," he said. He went to the record player and chose a song. "This is important. Always carry your own music." Hypnotic and compelling, Bob showed me poses to seduce the camera. Then he sat me down and showed me books with pictures from his favorite photographers, the ones who inspired him—from Alfred Stieglitz, Jacques Henri Lartigue, Bill Brandt, Robert Doisneau, Manuel Álvarez Bravo, and George Brassaï to the fashion photographers Horst, Cecil Beaton, Richard Avedon, and Irving Penn. He gave me a list of photographers I should work with, starting with Helmut Newton and ending with Guy Bourdin. "Stick with me," he said. "We'll show them."

For four years I went in and out of the light with Bob. He was crazy and troubled and fierce, but he was an amazing teacher. In times of unity, we had a strong collaboration. He taught me about timing, movement, what the camera sees. If it was there to steal your soul, well, he aimed to do just that—the conversation was seductive and the lens was a catalyst. But in order for us to live together, I had to believe that it was him and me against the world.

We had very little money. One option that we hadn't explored in New York was the infamous Chelsea Hotel, through the years a refuge of sorts for artists and drifters. It smelled of bad luck. It was the place where Dylan Thomas was staying when he died of pneumonia on November 9, 1953, and where, later, Nancy Spungen, the girlfriend of Sid Vicious of the Sex Pistols, was found stabbed to death on October 12, 1978. I don't mean to denigrate it as just a graveyard; living at the Chelsea Hotel was a rite of passage. From the moment you walked through the double doors into the lobby, you were on your way down the rabbit hole. "Red," the doorman and night porter, an older black man with orange hair and freckled skin, showed you to your room with an air of uncertainty and a rattling of keys. One felt lucky if it was unoccupied; half the time it seemed like the management didn't know. But in effect they had a point, as when the moment one entered, a thousand cockroaches revealed themselves, frozen in the sudden glare of the electric light. I hated them with a passion—their transparent bodies, their feelers testing the atmosphere, hiding in the dark cracks of the room, waiting for the darkness to manifest so they could reemerge to creep onto your pillow as you slept.

One night Bob and I came back to the room from the cinema. I was wearing the red fox fur coat that Marianne Faithfull had given to me as a parting gift in London. The sleeves were tight, so in order to take it off, I was pulling at some rings I was wearing. As Bob and I were talking, the closet door opened and a youngish man, dirty blond and strung out, pulled a straight-edged razor on us. "Tie her up!" he screamed. He ranted about how evil women were, chattel for the corporations, pigs that should be eradicated. During this diatribe, he wielded the razor, waving it about with abandon. Quietly and calmly, Bob sat down, raised his open hands as if in a blessing, and said gently, "I understand, you need help. Take what you need and leave." The intruder made a few more threats, then seemed to take stock and calmed down.

After severing the telephone cords and promising to cut our throats if we called the management, he grabbed my rings, took the key, fled the room, and locked us in from the outside. I had to climb across the outer balconies on the fifth floor to knock on the window of a lonely hippie girl in a bedroom. "Oh yeah, come in," she said tolerantly, without batting an eyelash. "This happens all the time at the Chelsea."

When we reported the incident, two cops came up to our room to take a statement, to examine the telephone cord, to touch Marianne's fur coat. They asked if I'd go along with them to the second floor, accompanied by Red, and proceeded to unlock a number of doors with a skeleton key. When I asked them about the logic of this, they explained that at the Chelsea, the perpetrator easily could turn out to be a patron. We didn't find him. Later I saw more of the inner lives of the hotel, including a bearded man in an all-white room with only newspapers and a bowl of goldfish for company, and an apartment on the top floor that seemed to be lined with bricks of hashish.

The artist Richard Bernstein lived at the Chelsea and was just starting to illustrate the covers of *Interview* magazine. His best friend was Berry Berenson, my friend from long-ago vacations in Klosters, now a photographer. She shot one of the first color covers of the magazine—a picture of me holding a microphone in one hand and a cigarette in the other; I must have said the word "groovy" fifty times in the article. I loved Berry. She had unique style and class. She was an American exotic—green eyes, honey skin, hair cut close. Soon she was to interview Tony Perkins for *Interview,* fall in love with him, marry him, and have two sons, Oz and Elvis. She was often at Halston's taking photographs. Andy Warhol's muse Viva was living at the Chelsea. She was quite beautiful in an emaciated way, with a long nose, heavy-lidded eyes, and a slow, stoned drawl. And there was Gerard Malanga, a dark, handsome poet with bad skin, who would hand me poems surreptitiously in the elevator. One of the mysteries of the Chelsea that I never solved was why there were gray footprints on the ceiling of our room.

I never felt so fragile or vulnerable as when Bob became demonic and flew into a rage, or worse, when afterward he retreated into his shell. One morning, four days into one of these ordeals, I

219

walked into our bathroom at the Chelsea and, in desperation, drew a razor blade across my left wrist. I ran back into the bedroom, blood spurting from the vein, crying to him, "Will this make you love me?" Bob came to, applied a tourniquet, and took me to the nearest emergency ward. The doctor stitched up my wrist without anesthesia, looked at me suspiciously, and asked me a lot of questions. I claimed I had fallen while carrying a knife. Later, when I told Bob I could not live like this anymore, he decided we should go on vacation. We were under too much stress, he said; we needed some sun.

Bob chose the small town of Zihuatanejo in southern Mexico, on the Mexican Pacific Costa Grande. Lauren Hutton had recommended it. We were to stay at the Hotel Caraçol, some two hundred steps up a cliff from the beach—a horseshoe of sand under the cover of a green mountain populated with little houses, mostly beach shacks and vacation homes for hippies. On the bay, a hefty-looking vessel—which we joked could be one of Richard Nixon's warships—idled out in deep water. On our first day in town, we met some students and shared a joint with them. We asked if they knew where we could get some grass.

That night a man came to the door with a one-pound paper sack of marijuana. Bob and I were having a disagreement of some sort and didn't invite him in. Bob paid the man and he left. We smoked a spliff and the mood changed between us. Suddenly, we were happy and laughing. We decided to skip down to the beach at sunset for a swim in what looked to be a warm, inviting ocean. As we passed a group of soldiers, Federales, sitting by the seawall, we wished them a good evening. Gingerly, we made our way barefoot across a mound of rocks and through a tide pool to a second beach that ended in a cluster of black rocks, a promontory that jutted into the bay. Here we undressed, smoked the rest of the joint, and swam happily in the dark waters for some ten to fifteen minutes. When we emerged dripping onto the beach, something brushed against me, and I made out the shapes of more than a few men moving toward us in the dusk. By now I had four gun barrels trained on my torso. Back and front. "Put on your robe," Bob whispered after he realized that we were not alone. Silently, I obeyed him.

One of the Federales had a flashlight and was examining the contents of Bob's bathrobe pockets. He came up with the key to our room. "We are American tourists," said Bob, grabbing back the key. All I could think of was the pound of grass in the closet. Finally, the soldier gestured for us to walk on in front of them, in the direction of the hotel. He began to speak in Spanish on a walkie-talkie, but as we walked up the beach ahead of their guns, they began to overtake us, forcing us into the surf. It was a dark, moonless evening. A searchlight came on, shining from the mountain above, trailing up and down the sand like something out of a war movie, followed by a black-out in the village. Another spotlight, from the Nixon warship, burned a white hole through the night. The Federales began to load their rifles; by now they were surrounding us in a semi-circle. Their leader called out something in Spanish and the men lifted their rifles.

I tried to scream for help, but the sound was smothered by my throat constricting and came out as a yelp. We were clearly about to be murdered. The soldier's radio started to crackle, and Bob grabbed me by the hair. "Hit the dirt," he said, pushing me down. I sank to my knees in the surf and watched in terror as the searchlights played on the surface of the water. The men lowered their guns. There was chatter among them. Some started to move off toward the jungle. Bob pulled me up from the water. "Run," he told me, and like an Olympian, I flew down the beach in front of him, fully expecting to get shot in the back, scaling in one fell swoop the rocks it had previously taken us five minutes to negotiate.

As we turned the corner of the street leading to the hotel, a flashlight shone directly in our faces. For a moment, I thought all was lost. But as we moved past, we realized it was only an elderly Mexican gentleman out with his dog in the darkness. He laughed at us, and we ran on until we reached our room, gasping. Later that night I tiptoed out to the building site behind the hotel and flung the bag of grass as far as I could into some weeds. The next morning I tried to book a plane out, but there were no flights for four days. Bob and I were like caged lions again. I was afraid to leave the hotel by night for the rest of our time there, and pondered whether it was worth it to retrieve the pot. Ultimately, I decided against it.

The Mexico trip seemed to provide more evidence that wherever we went and whatever we did held the possibility of disaster. It only strengthened Bob's conviction that the world was his enemy. And I, trapped psychologically and physically, burdened by my connection and responsibility to him, had become isolated from my friends and family and found myself sinking into the misery that was suffocating him.

From John Huston
October 23, 1970

Darling daughter,

You're right. I'm deplorable as a correspondent. No question where you got it from. Your lovely letter has gone hand-to-hand down the line, through Glades and B. O'K [Betty O'Kelly] and Nurse to the kitchen and finally the yard. All hearts were made glad. Likewise, yours to Allegra. I'm sure she answered by return mail, punctilious as she is. Pity you can't get her newly acquired accent from the written word. It's the despair of B. O'K who tends to admire things English. In any case, Allegra is now talking like a stage Colleen and rather more Irish than the Lynches. But she is in splendid form. No more circles under the eyes, has stand up brawls, sheds few tears when she falls off her bicycle, and makes the meadows ring with laughter. She's not the horsewoman her sister was at that age, but considerably more studious. She devours everything in print and is so good at cards, I'm thinking of taking her to the Claremont and backing her game. If only Lord Darby played Old Maid.

Tony is in London—well established in his flat, surrounded by his collections. He too, is in great form, the best I've ever seen him. He's a joy to be with. An extraordinary companion. We're going on a trip in a few days to the Rothschilds in the South of France, then on to Spain and Italy. I bought some land in Italy. It's between Rome and Florence and perfectly beautiful. If Tony really likes it, I'm going to help him put up a house on it.

I've two pictures lined up, one—the first—to be made in Spain, and the other in California. I start shooting January 4. Is there any chance of you and Bob coming over for Christmas? You're much wanted. I see you in Vogue—looking wonderful. I've been painting quite a lot. There are about fifteen canvases now you haven't seen. There's talk about an exhibition. I don't know—maybe it's better to keep at least that part of my life exceedingly private. Only for relatives and close friends. The well disposed.

Seamus and Shu-Shu and Simba and Frisco, Kildare and the three thoroughbred mares and their three foals are all thriving. There has been one addition—ducks. A present of eight, from Kevin MacClorey. They perform amazing aerobatics in the river all day, then, when dusk comes on, they come up out of the water,

line up, and march off single-filed to their house behind the barn.
Two muscovys, six Indian runners, if you know your ducks.

I was in Africa for a month for a film on the preservation of
wildlife—appearing, not directing, in Kenya with the wardens
of the national parks—great game sanctuaries. It was a splen-
did experience altogether. They—the wardens—are an extraor-
dinary breed, quite the best men I've met in years. I could go on
about Africa and them and on and on. The best thing I can say
about them is I envy them. The show will appear on the American
Sportsman Program sometime early next year. I don't know how
good it will be, but it should have some unique scenes. I've never
been photographed being charged by an elephant before.

The days are dwindling—but then it's almost November. The
avenue is carpeted with leaves. The rain is a cold rain. And the sun
is a pale sun. The opening meet was day before yesterday. Nothing
memorable occurred. Lots of falls, as usual, on the first official day, but
no casualties. Lady Ampthill has retired from the field. Times toll.

Much Love, my Blessed One. And love to Bob, who from the
way you sound, must be taking very good care of you indeed.

As ever,
Dad

In 1971 Bob and I decided to move to Paris. We loved to shoot
for Dior with the great makeup artist and perfume designer
Serge Lutens, whose extraordinary talent and eye for detail
inspired us. Working for the European magazines was liberat-
ing in terms of content and expression. We shot for *Elle*, British *Vogue*, French *Vogue*, Italian *Vogue*, *Nova*, *Harpers & Queen*,
and many others. Posing for Bob's camera was like acting in a
movie, and we always had a background idea or story.

Serge was a legend as a makeup artist and already a mysterious and rare commodity in the beauty industry. He lived in Paris at no fixed address. When French *Vogue* wanted to book him for a feature, scouts were sent out all over the city to find him. Generally he could be located at his favorite table at the Café de Flore. Serge was like a nocturnal animal, with great dark eyes. He wore his jet-black hair straight, in a Dutch-boy haircut, under a John Lennon cap. He didn't speak a word of English, but it never mattered, because the language between Bob and Serge was aesthetic. It was a great feeling to be the muse between them. At this time, Serge gave me the haircut that became my trademark—full bangs and dead straight, to just below the ears, like the silent-movie star Louise Brooks. It was to change my life as a model.

Bob and I had no friends to speak of in Paris, other than a few of his ex-models, one a beautiful girl called Ingemarie with whom I guessed he might have had an affair in the past; Joan Buck; and a photographer called Tony Kent, who had a big apartment in the 16th arrondissement where we sometimes stayed. Tony was also a good friend of Norma's. He used to ride all over Paris on a high-handled bike like the Harley in *Easy Rider.* Through him and his wife, Susan, I met a lovely American girl, Phyllis Major, who was dating Warren Beatty.

> From John Huston at the Alhambra
> Palace Hotel, Granada, Spain
> January 27, 1971
> To Anjelica at the Hôtel Esméralda, Paris

Darling daughter,
How good to know you're geographically near again. When the picture is finished I'll come by Paris and we'll all have a time—

Tony and Glades too of course, and perhaps Allegra. I've been promising her a trip if she learned French and from all reports, colored of course, she's practically bilingual. I've put St. Clerans up for sale. Sad but necessary. The expense of running the place has more than trebled in the last few years, so it's a luxury no longer to be afforded. I have to stay away making pictures to earn enough to keep it going, a vicious circle.

Are you and Bob well acquainted in Paris? I know a lot of people from its various worlds that you might care to meet—Rothschilds, Anouile, Suzanne et al—but I won't write them unless you tell me to.

This is my first extended time in Spain and I'm thoroughly enjoying it. The Spaniards themselves are singularly attractive, a Latin version of the Irish, a combination of elegance and primitiveness, trusting and touchy. Knowing the Mexicans as I do, it's fascinating to meet up with their antecedents.

We had a bullfight scene in the film and your brother, acting on inspiration, leaped into the ring and faced the bull with a cape. He made several passes with the cape and was only mildly bumped. The onlookers were lavish with their olés, and the scene ended with Tony being borne aloft on the shoulders of the crowd.

Do you get multicolored letters from Allegra? She writes me regularly in a fastidious hand in a variety of inks. She seems very happy. You might, if you have a spare weekend, run over. She'd love to see you and so would I.

Much love to Bob.

As ever,
Dad

When Dad wrote to tell me that he was putting St. Clerans up for sale, it was already a fait accompli. He had not asked

Tony or me for our counsel or input or even our feelings on the matter. I was speechless and didn't write back to Dad about the impending sale of my childhood home. Gladys was taking care of his business affairs, as usual. He had already sold much of the art and furniture to personal collectors and museums and through auction houses. Tony and I had always assumed that St. Clerans would be ours forever, especially when Dad referred to Tony as "my son and heir." I believe that it broke Tony's heart, as it did mine, when St. Clerans went. And if Dad's heart was broken, he didn't share that information with us. As the Irish say, Dad gave up the ghost when he let go of St. Clerans.

Bob and I worked on some remarkable shoots in Europe. One for Valentino in Rome, which attracted a good deal of attention, was an homage to Luchino Visconti's film *The Damned*. It involved a series of photographs for Italian *Vogue* of me and a male model, Lipp Jens, dressed as a Nazi, posing at various locations, including the Borghese Gardens and the Termini train station. We did a story for French *Vogue* in Ireland during a particularly intense period of IRA violence, for which Bob photographed me on the Sarsfield Bridge at St. Clerans, with a shotgun by my side and a bullet hole above my heart. On another sitting for French *Vogue,* I wandered the aisles of the brasserie La Coûpole in hot pants and a huge black picture hat, in floods of tears. The diners kept taking pity on me and tried to get me to share their meals. It was actually very sweet.

Bob and I were at our happiest when we were working together, and getting wages for doing what we loved helped alleviate the stresses in our relationship. But it took at least three months for Bob to be paid by the magazines, and although we also worked for advertisers, those bookings were less frequent. One morning as we were sitting outside the Café de Flore in St. Germain, I saw a familiar face across the street. It was my Rhodesian friend Jeremy Railton, whom I hadn't seen since he left London to become a stage designer in Los Angeles. Our eyes met. I couldn't tell him at the time, but I knew that merely recognizing him would probably lead to some unpleasantness, some manifestation of jealousy or insecurity, on Bob's part. So I nodded perfunctorily and widened my eyes in a warning for him not to come any closer. He got the message and moved on down the sidewalk. I felt that my real life was slipping away.

At the spring collections in Paris, I was working with Guy Bourdin at the *Vogue* studios in the Place du Palais Bourbon. Gil of Max Factor—I never came to know his surname—was doing my makeup, and I was very unhappy. Guy had told everyone that he wanted the models to look fresh-faced and all-American. This was decidedly not my look. Gil was painting my eyelids turquoise when I spoke up; the tension had been building in me, and I began to cry uncontrollably. The two other models working in the studio, Wallis Franken and Tracy Weed, lifted me up and carried me out of the dressing room to walk me around the square, one under each arm.

I guess I was having a full-on nervous breakdown. When I stopped choking on my tears, they brought me back to the studio. Guy, who spoke very little as a rule, asked what was going on. I replied that I was ugly—my eyes too small, my nose too big—and that the makeup was not helping. Guy pondered this statement for a little while and said, "If your eyes are small, then we should make them smaller, and likewise, if your nose is big, we have to make it larger. You think these are your failings, but it is just the opposite."

I went back to the makeup chair. My eyes were swollen from crying. "How do you want to look?" asked Gil of Max Factor.

"Make her look like a vampire," Guy said. This worked beautifully for us both, and we ended around midnight in high spirits. When I walked into Tony Kent's apartment, where Bob and I were staying, the phone was ringing. It was an editor at *Vogue.* She asked if I could return to the Place du Palais Bourbon. "It's for the lead page," she said. "Helmut Newton is photographing."

This was music to my ears. I called a taxi and went back to the 7th arrondissement. It was three in the morning. The famous Mr. Newton was standing in the dark, naked street, with one light and a Polaroid camera. I had heard that he was mean to girls, and that he was scary to work for, but my experience was just the opposite. He photographed me stalking the pavement, the red flash reflecting in my eyes like something out of *Night of the Living Dead,* as he called out instructions—"Faster! Slower! Head up! March!"—until dawn broke over Paris.

I often made the trip across the border to Milan. The overnight train compartments were perfectly designed, with mahogany interiors and a little sink in the corner for ablutions; the windows actually opened. I loved lying in the dark under a crisp cotton duvet, watching the snow-covered fields almost phosphorescent under a white moon, falling asleep to the motion of the train, as we powered forward through the night. Out of Bob's orbit, my mind would wander back in time to my former life, to Mum, and to all that I had left behind.

I usually traveled to Milan to work with either of my two favorite photographers in Italy, Gian Paolo Barbieri or Alfa Castaldi. Alfa was married to the brilliantly bizarre editor of Italian *Vogue,* Anna Piaggi. Alfa and Anna had met in Rome during the Second World War, when she worked for the food section of a popular newspaper and he was a staff photographer. Alfa told me Anna would cook these amazing meals that he would photograph in the most romantic light, and then they would sit down and eat. That was how they fell in love. Anna lived and breathed extreme fashion, and the times I spent in Alfa's studio, eating fresh mozzarella and salad in the afternoon before starting a night's work, are some of my happiest memories from that time.

It was, however, always a slightly traumatic affair to be working in Italy, because we didn't have permits. Unless we were lucky enough to be put up at the Grand Hotel, the models usually wound up staying at one of the smaller places in town, like the Hotel Arena, and every so often the police would do a swoop, and all the girls who didn't have papers would be paddy-wagoned off to the train station. Naturally, the girls would disembark at the next stop and make their way back to Milan, but it was inconvenient. A lot of girls were underage, and you'd see these little blonds in the lobby, sweet and fresh from Denmark and Sweden. Some of them were supplementing their income by going on "dates" with the local businessmen. I remember one of these girls in the lobby of the Arena, looking like a wet kitten in a sodden fur coat, dripping from head to toe. Her date hadn't liked her attitude, so he had held her under a cold shower.

Usually, the booking agency—in my case a company called Models International—controlled the payments. They had agencies in both Paris and Milan, and every Friday there was a long line of girls waiting to collect their checks at the accounting window before the agency closed down for the weekend. If you arrived too late, the window would shut in your face. After one such Friday, I left Paris with no extra money in my purse. I picked up my prepaid ticket for the train to Milan from the Gare du Nord and went straight to work with Alfa. It was a long day, and as a sweet gesture, the designer Mario Valentino gave me a pair of shoes I'd admired, with six-inch silver heels, which I put on immediately. I was to collect my fee from the Milan agency that night in cash, and go directly back to Paris.

I took a taxi to the office. When I asked for my check in halting Italian, they stared at me blankly. "No," they said, they didn't owe me any money, and after all, who had paid the train fare? It was understood that if a client brought you in from Paris, the travel would be covered. I pleaded with them and told them I had no money. They gave me a map and instructed me to go to a train station where a prepaid ticket would be waiting for me. Naturally, when the taxi got to the station, I had barely enough money to pay the fare. When I asked for the last train to Paris, they told me I was at the wrong station. A ticket master took pity on me, drove me fast across town, and dropped me in the main square close to the terminal. By now I was limping in the six-inch heels, struggling to balance on the cobblestones. It was cold and night was falling.

As I made my way forward to the ticket booth, my heart was in my mouth. What if they had not prepaid the ticket? I knew that Bob was in the same position I was, broke, in Paris. He wouldn't be able to bail me out.

"No, signorina, no prepaid ticket."

I began to cry. I had nowhere to go, no one to ask for help. The situation was hopeless. A gentleman turned to me. "Take my ticket," he said, pressing it into my hand. "My wife will be happy I did not leave tonight." This was a miraculous incident, though it did not reassure me that all was going to work out blissfully. As much as Bob wanted control, he was unable to protect me.

We lived in a series of hotels, each room more modest than the last. It was possible to exist in Paris on very little money, yet we were always low on funds. Joan Buck, who had been working as a stylist for Guy Bourdin before we came to Paris, was going on location as a freelance fashion editor for the magazine *Vingt Ans* and offered us the apartment she had been renting on the rue du Bac. I placed my suitcases in a corridor outside the apartment in a storage closet with a padlock on the door. Stupidly, I had not imagined that anyone would try to break in. Almost everything I owned was stolen, including the watch I had bought Mum from Cartier and all of Bob's cameras and lenses. I called Dad's lawyer, Henry Hyde, and asked if I could withdraw some money from my Swiss bank account to get to England. To do me the favor, he charged almost as much as I withdrew.

I did not enjoy being broke. In my heart, I knew that if things got really dire, I could go to Dad. But I was convinced that the only way to retain my power with him was not to ask for money. I did not want him to have an advantage over Bob and me.

Later that year, when I was booked to do runway work for the designer Zandra Rhodes in London, Bob and I moved into a bed-sit in Ladbroke Grove, a room with worn brown carpet and a gas meter that you had to put shillings into for heat. If there hadn't been a trace of the ridiculous about this tragically shabby downgrade, I might have despaired. At one point finding ourselves without the cash to buy our next meal, I called Mum's old friend Peter Menegas to ask him for a small loan. He came over to the bed-sit with a bag of groceries in his arms and gave me ten pounds. It felt like winning the lottery. And it was true that with the next check cashed by Bob with the Bank of England, our circumstances changed and we were relatively happy, ensconced at Cyril Mansions, Prince of Wales Drive, Battersea, in a cozy flat sublet to us by a model called Vicki Howard. But there were always the black moods, the silences, the accusations, the isolation of Bob's world.

It was around this time that Bob first said he wanted me to have a baby; he asked whether I was taking birth control. Why wasn't I getting pregnant? Indeed, I had stopped taking birth control and had not become pregnant. He told me I wasn't a real woman. "Real women get pregnant and raise children," he said. I remembered the flash pains in my lower abdomen that had taken my breath away in the back of the taxicab with my mother in London.

I went to a gynecologist, who told me they would have to operate in order to find the obstruction. I refused to have surgery. In my heart I was very afraid to have a child. Woman or not. I realized that in order to find out why I was not becoming pregnant, I would have to become so. Although I thought there was a possibility that such an undertaking might change Bob for the better and make him a transformed and happy man, I also knew that, at twenty years old, I was not ready to be a mother and that having his child would tie me to him forever. I was not ready for that, either.

The one thing I loved more than anything was doing shows. Zandra Rhodes had booked me through Eileen Green, my lovely new Irish agent in London. Zandra was a joy to work for. The first time I did a show for her, the girls walked up and down a spiral staircase at a boutique called Piero di Monzi on the Fulham Road. It was always a treat to wear her clothes, the most romantic of the period, and Zandra was a wonderful bird of paradise herself, with all these different colors in her hair and a thick Cockney accent.

The Japanese designer Kansai Yamamoto put on an extraordinary first show in London. The girls had pen-and-ink drawings painted on their bodies by a master tattoo artist. Kansai had imported some fantastic exotics for the runway—among them, for the first time ever in England, the Hawaiian beauty Marie Helvin, later one of England's top models and a bride and muse of David Bailey's.

The girls were fabulous, and we all got along really well. I can't remember a single bad moment or catfight. On the contrary, we were always supportive of one another. I remember an amazing zaftig blond model of Helmut Newton's, a cool German called Mercedes, who tucked me under her arm in Rome when I was lonely at the Grand Hotel; Tracy Weed and Wallis, who dried my tears when I broke down with self-loathing and fatigue at collection week in Paris; and Marie Helvin, who made ramen for her sister and me in her little flat in Knightsbridge.

When Bob and I moved back to New York, an apartment came up for rent in Gramercy Park. It was in a white building with yellow windows near the Arts Club, at 13 Gramercy Park South, across from the hotel. The apartment was a large studio overlooking the gardens, adjacent to where Susan Forristal, a beautiful Irish Texan whom Bob often paired with me in photographs, lived with her boyfriend, Allan. We were friends, and she was one of the very few people of whom Bob approved. He photographed us together quite often for Saks Fifth Avenue campaign ads. Susan and I had found some spectacular lace curtains on an outing to an antique shop, and, true to my usual style, they were almost the only items of furnishing in the apartment.

Allegra and Nurse were spending some time with Grandpa and Nana on Long Island. Allegra was a beautiful six-year-old and looked like Alice in Wonderland. But she was solemn and I was concerned for her. I could see that even though Nurse had remained with her faithfully, she missed Mum deeply. There was talk of Allegra remaining with the Somas, though I had not heard from Dad what his intentions were for her in the fall. It was evident to me that our grandparents were a bit too far along to take care of her. Grandpa was in his eighties, and Nana had her hands full just looking after him. Grandpa had shingles, was getting progressively senile, and had become obsessed with the evils of gambling. Decisions needed to be made about the future of my little sister. In the interim, when she came to New York, I would take her for ice cream at Serendipity or shopping at Saks.

On alternate weekends, Norma would bring Terry down from Woodstock to stay with Bob and me. He was a year younger than Allegra, a cherubic child with olive skin and blond curls, quiet and thoughtful. I could tell that he liked me but took it hard that I had come between his parents. Even though I felt that Norma looked at me with contempt for stealing her husband, I could also feel her pity for me. On one occasion, she and I had a face-off after she dropped Terry at the apartment.

"You poor idiot child," she said, lighting her cigarette, taking a deep drag, and throwing the match casually into a basket of firelighters and kindling by the side of the mantelpiece. "You understand nothing!" Norma had an Eskimo face with pale blue eyes and a cloud of fair hair; she looked like Little Orphan Annie.

I strode across the room and grabbed her hair in one hand and opened the front door with the other in a rather deft move. "Don't come back till you apologize," I said, and shut the door.

Surprisingly, after this incident, Norma and I became friends. Later that year, when her divorce from Bob came through, she met an English musician called Jackie Lomax. She changed her name to Annie when she married him.

Not long after our return to New York, my bookings began to fall off again, with no interest from advertising at all. I asked Eileen Ford why she thought I was not working, and she suggested I get a nose job. I went crying to Bob. "You've already worked with the best in the world," he said. "Me and Avedon." I soon left Ford, and when I transferred to Wilhelmina, I found out that Dick Avedon had a hand in preventing other photographers from working with me at *Vogue,* by insisting that I be exclusive to him.

Fortunately, everyone loved my French haircut, I was good on the runway, and I started to work for Halston. Halston's shows were famous not only for the clothes but for the versatility of the girls. We called ourselves "the Halstonettes." Pat Cleveland usually opened the show. A unique model, she looked like a sister to the late Josephine Baker and had legs as tall as the Empire State Building. There was Heidi Goldberg, a small, angelic blond; Karen Bjornson, Halston's muse and house model; Elsa Peretti, who went on to be the top designer at Tiffany & Co.; Beverly Johnson, a ravishing black woman who helped break the mold; Naty Abascal, who looked like a flamenco dancer; Pilar Crespi, a beautiful society girl—each one fabulously different. As his signature, Halston would bring out Pat Ast, who weighed over three hundred pounds and had frizzy henna-red hair, dancing down the catwalk in a printed caftan and waving a Japanese fan, and everyone would go mad. Joe Eula drew illustrations of us all, and the film director Joel Schumacher was a fixture backstage, as were Berry Berenson and Stephen Sprouse. I used to play around a bit and change up the pace when I was walking on the runway, catch someone's eye, to have some fun with it and break up the monotony of just stalking up and down with a vacant look on my face. I guess that's supposed to make you look at the clothes, but I always end up looking at the models. I loved the catwalk, and it provided a somewhat pleasant and safe respite from acting.

Halston was cool, chic, and slender in black cashmere, calmly sitting behind his desk in his mirrored beige office, but, as I was to discover, occasionally a little snippy when warming up for a show. On my first outing for him, I thought I'd done well, but he took me aside and said rather caustically, "The Halston woman doesn't raise her arms above her head." The next day there was an article about me in the *New York Post* by Eugenia Sheppard, very nice, with photographs and one large picture with my arms in the air. "I was mistaken—you can do what you like with your arms," Halston said to me with a wink.

I had great respect for Halston, as did all his girls. He had a big hand in bringing chic to the American woman; his choices were always simple and totally luxurious, and working for him was a privilege. I stopped modeling before all the craziness of the late seventies and early eighties, when everyone was spending their nights clubbing at Studio 54. Even before the scourge of AIDS and the brilliant lives it destroyed, many people whom I loved and collaborated with died. They were playing loose and fast with drugs, altering their moods to match the whimsy of the time.

Nobody ate then, the models least of all. I would carry around a six-pack of Coca-Cola and store it in the refrigerator of any studio where I was working. I remember going to Grist-edes and buying frozen meals, like chicken potpie or potatoes au gratin. It was another state and time from the dinners that I would help Mum prepare in London, chopping the parsley and peeling the garlic, or eating from the garden in faraway Ireland.

CHAPTER 16

Anjelica in Co. Clare, Ireland, 1971

On one occasion in Paris, Bob had introduced me to Dr. Pierre Bensousan, the French doctor he credited with saving him from a serious addiction to speed in the early sixties. Dr. Bensousan had put Bob on a "sleeping cure" by administering sodium pentothal. Bob had been introduced to amphetamine in New York by a man he described as both a brilliant scientist and a sociopath—a Dr. Max Jacobson, dubbed by his patients "Miracle Max" or "Dr. Feelgood," who, under the pretext of helping Bob with his affliction, did the opposite by injecting him with a heady cocktail of speed and vitamins. Soon he became addicted. Dr. Jacobson's most famous patient was rumored to have been John F. Kennedy.

In 1972 Bob received a call from the *New York Times*. The newspaper had decided to do an exposé in light of Dr. Jacobson's nefarious practices and roster of star patients. It was an illustrious group consisting of many famous people, from Margot Fonteyn and her husband—Roberto Arias, Panama's ambassador to the United Kingdom—to Prince Stanislaw "Stash" Radziwill, Anthony Quinn, Truman Capote, Alan J. Lerner, Eddie Fisher, Tennessee Williams, and the *Life* and Kennedy White House photographer Mark Shaw, who was found later with a needle in his arm, dead from chronic amphetamine poisoning. As a result of the inquest, Dr. Jacobson's New York State medical license was revoked in 1975.

I guess someone must have given the article to Dad, who called in an understanding and benevolent mood to ask me to come see him at the St. Regis Hotel. He was passing through New York on his way from Ireland to Los Angeles. When I went up to the suite, Dad greeted me affectionately and casually dropped the news that he was getting married. He neither showed me a photograph nor described the woman, other than to mention that she lived in Los Angeles, her name was Celeste Shane, and she was called Cici. While this announcement came as a surprise, my first reaction was relief that the meeting was about his impending marriage and did not focus on me.

Before Dad left town for the coast the next day, he visited us at Gramercy Park. It was to be his first meeting with Bob. When

I nervously opened the door, Dad was standing in the hall in a gray tweed overcoat with a Sherlock Holmes cape lined in brown velvet, looking like he'd just blown in from Co. Mayo. He was bearded and wearing a cloth cap. He entered the living room and shook hands with Bob. The meeting was something of an anticlimax. I had half expected Dad to murder Bob on sight, but the atmosphere was mercifully devoid of drama.

There was little furniture, no chair to sit on, just a queen-size bed in front of a white marble fireplace, its mantel adorned with my usual large arrangement of lilies, gladioli, and snapdragons. Dad was upbeat, almost jovial. "Well, isn't this nice," he said, looking around. "You have to come out to L.A. to meet Cici, and then we'll go on a fishing trip to Cabo San Lucas. There's great fishing in the Sea of Cortez." Bob and I agreed that this was a wonderful idea. I knew that Dad and Bob would never be friends. Not in a million years. Dad departed soon after. He didn't stay for the pot roast I'd cooked for him; he left with a sweep of the cape, taking with him the energy he'd brought to the room. Together, Bob and I heaved a sigh of relief.

Work continued to fluctuate. Either we were shooting for the top magazines or not employed at all. Although we needed the money, my jobs with other photographers became increasingly difficult for Bob to accept. He would rip them apart, pointing out their every weakness. I fully understood at this point that in Bob's view, there was "them" and there was "us," and anything could tip the balance.

Most dreadful of Bob's moods were the silences, when he would turn his face to the wall, staring vacantly. These episodes lasted up to three or four days. I would attempt to communicate with him, but he would refuse to speak. When he returned from his absent state, it was usually to ask for food. Bob was often volatile around meals. On one occasion he demanded steak and when I served it to him he threw it across the room, claiming that it had taken too long to cook. He became furious if I didn't shop for meat daily.

One night after a terrible scene, I ran away from the apartment and went to see a male model with whom I had worked on a number of occasions. I slept with him, but he talked about his ex-girlfriend, a model called Ali McGraw, for most of the night. When I went home to Bob in the morning and told him what had happened, he seemed strangely accepting of the events and acknowledged that he had driven me away. Instead of attempting to kill me, he reacted with equanimity. Just when you thought you had a handle on Bob, he would change colors. I could never anticipate his plunges into the emotional abyss or accept that I didn't have the power to dispel his demons.

A month or so after Dad's visit to New York, Bob and I flew to California for the fishing trip in La Paz. It was March. The West Coast was green and sunny and the air smelled sweet, like jasmine. After the grayness of New York, I thought it was blissful. We stayed the night in Cici's Pacific Palisades house, which Dad now shared.

Cici was a tawny-haired beauty in her mid-thirties, outspoken and informal; she dressed in caftans and seemed relaxed and at ease. When she smiled, her mouth squared off at the corners and she spoke in an affable drawl. She introduced us to her son, Collin, whose father was the screenwriter Walon Green. Her home was a single-story ranch house with a simple floor plan—a lot of glass, and sea-grass matting on the floor, like Dad's loft in Ireland. I wondered if this was his influence. I also recognized some of the items from St. Clerans in the mix—the wood-and-plaster mermaids from the upstairs landing, a circlet of Etruscan gold as fragile as feathers that had lived in a glass cabinet in his vestibule, the card table with its inlaid rose, ring, and dagger from the Red Sitting Room. In Cici's house, it all looked like pirate treasure plundered from the mother ship.

When Dad had taken Cici on her first visit to St. Clerans, she'd had a nasty confrontation with Betty, who had retreated to her parents' home in Co. Kildare. Cici had inspected the house-keeping ledgers and made discoveries of improper payments and excessive salaries to the staff. St. Clerans was, as she described it to me later, "a useless heap." It may have been Dad's intention to sell St. Clerans in any case. The expense of the place and the cold, damp climate were weighing on him.

Now he told me that the Monet had sold to Houston's Museum of Fine Arts and that the house was being dismantled. He said, "Select one thing from the house, one thing you would like to have." I could tell that the fantasy had died for him. The dream had shattered.

I chose a little Rodin sculpture that had lived on the mantel-piece in the drawing room. A man, woman, and child molded as one in bronze, the perfect family that never was. For me it sym-bolized the thing I had wanted most as a child—for my parents to love each other and be together. With the abandonment of St. Clerans, all that had belonged to us, all that we felt was ours, was sold, scattered, and squandered. I didn't talk to Tony about this. I am not sure what he was doing at this time; probably he had met Margot Cholmondeley, his future wife and later the mother of three of his children. I do not believe that Dad gave Tony the same consolation prize that he offered me.

Without delay, we flew to La Paz the following morning. We were met by a driver who took us a long way down to the tip of Baja in a tour van, past miles of deserted coastline bordered by jungle and old palm trees. We stopped for lunch at a hotel and ate rice and beans alongside the residents, at a long refectory table in a dining room that felt like an army mess hall. After lunch we continued on past more brackish landscape to reach our final destination, a hotel with a forlorn row of condominiums on a stark yellow beach, next to a tuna cannery. It looked the way I imagined Algeria looked in the fifties. Down on the ocean, a few rusty white fishing boats bobbed alongside a concrete pier, and the smells of petrol and decaying fish were pungent on the dry, hot night air. Seemingly, we were the only guests. We were shown to our rooms, two duplex apartments side by side, with paper-thin walls and a trickle of running water in the shower.

I speculated that Dad was laying down a blanket of complaint and criticism to Cici on the subject of Bob, although I couldn't decipher what was being said even when I put my ear to the wall. Our instructions from Dad were to freshen up and meet for a drink by the pool. Bob was already beginning to exhibit signs of stress; he declared as soon as we were alone that this felt nothing like a holiday. Nevertheless, we showered and heard their door slam as they made off to the bar. We ran to catch up. Dad was moving on long legs up the wooden slatted walkway, not a second to be wasted. At the otherwise deserted bar, on Bob's recommendation, I ordered a banana daiquiri, and he ordered one for himself. Dad looked at Bob from behind his cerveza the way a silverback looks at a tourist.

The call was for seven the following morning. We were to have coffee and eggs and hit the harbor at the crack of dawn in order to get a head start on the fishing. Marlin, described by Dad as the "king of the fighting fish," was the day's objective.

Cici and Dad had already finished their huevos rancheros by the time Bob and I arrived at the breakfast table. Our eggs were sitting, cold and oily, on plates in front of us. Dad was itching to get started, rising to move off as soon as we made our appearance. I had some suntan oil in my bag and little else, no hat and nothing to cover my shoulders or legs. I was wearing a bikini and was determined to get a tan to take back to New York. As we clambered onto the deck of the foul-smelling little fishing boat, I felt a wave of nausea and a stab of regret. Cici and Dad, speaking enthusiastic pidgin Spanish to a couple of boatmen who displayed little interest, were already flexing their fiberglass fishing rods and lowering themselves into two white plastic swiveling chairs on the back of the boat as, in a cloud of diesel, we putt-putted out to deeper waters.

No sooner had Cici cast out her line than a magnificent black sailfish took the bait and flew out of the boat's wake in the opening arabesque of a death dance. Cici reeled him in after a prolonged fight, and the boatmen netted him against the side of the boat, slicing at the long aquiline head with a machete. The dorsal fin a row of bloody quills, life deserting the rainbow skin, the shining black crest of muscle was carcass in minutes. By now the sun was climbing high in a cloudless sky, and land had left the horizon. We drifted on the waves for a while, and Dad and Cici cast more lines. Dad hooked a shark, hoping it was a marlin, and cut it loose. After nearly five hours, as the sun rose to its full zenith, he decided to call it a day and indicated for the boatmen to restart the engine, but it had gone dead.

Nothing they did seemed to work—the engine caught fire briefly, and we were enveloped in toxic smoke. For an hour or more we drifted in the oppressive glare of the afternoon. My skin was beginning to blister. The stench of petrol and dead fish was overwhelming. Black flies began to bite. The reluctant boatmen attempted to make contact on their radio and eventually another boat appeared and threw us a towline. It was sunset by the time we docked and weakly climbed the hill to the hotel bar. I asked for a strawberry daiquiri. Bob said, "You don't want that."

Dad cast a look in my direction. My face was swollen from sun poisoning. "She should have whatever she likes," he said quietly.

The next morning, Cici informed Bob and me at breakfast that Dad had left for La Paz. He wanted to have a look at property along the coast that he thought might be a good investment. She said that he was also going in search of a black pearl for me. He had told me the night before that when he first lived in Mexico, when he rode with the cavalry as a young man in his twenties, La Paz had been the center for black pearls. Because of his tradition of presenting me with important gems on special occasions, or maybe because he'd married Mum in La Paz, the quest to find a perfect black pearl had assumed great importance in his mind.

All day I lay indoors and nursed my sunburn. Bob went to lunch with Cici. When he came back, he said, "She was totally coming on to me." At dusk, I watched as Dad ambled stiffly down the wooden slats that led across the sand to the condominium. He carried two straw hats, one for Cici and one for me. He looked bone-tired.

"There are no pearls, black or white, left in La Paz," he said.

The next morning, however, Dad was again determined to examine the acres of beach we had passed on our way down the coast. With a full day to spare before our return to California, his plan was that we should drive back to La Paz and stay overnight in a motel. This time we had a Realtor in tow, and he parked the cars and walked us through the jungle down to the water. Dad was right; it was Eden—hundreds of miles of uninhabited beach. I often think that if we had followed his instinct, we would have bought a gold mine.

As soon as we reached town, Bob and I went for a swim in the pool at the motel. Then Dad called me into his room to discuss the property. I must have sat and talked with him for the better part of an hour. I was anxious to get back to Bob, because I had told him I would be with Dad for just ten minutes. When I returned to the pool, the shadows were long, and Bob had left the scene. I walked back to our room at the opposite end of the pool from Dad's. When I opened the door, a bottle of tequila narrowly missed my head and shattered on the wall behind me. I flew out the door and ran around the corner of the building. My heart was beating loud.

As I pressed my cheek against the plaster wall, I heard Al Green singing "Livin' for You" through an open window above my head. I did not have the courage to either reenter the room or go to Dad. Instead, I ran as fast as I could across the parking lot and down to the beach, where I fell to my knees on the sand and prayed to God for help. I was gagging for air. The beach was empty, but when I looked up, a red sun was setting behind a tall figure in the distance. As he drew closer, I saw that he was dark-skinned and dressed in white, a very beautiful-looking man in a serape and a wide straw hat. At a few yards away, our eyes met. He came closer. He crouched down on his heels and gazed deeply into my eyes for a long moment. My breath calmed and I stopped crying. He raised his hand and put it on my shoulder. I felt a wave of strength wash over me. He smiled and nodded. I nodded back. "Yes, I am all right."

He stood up and quietly moved on, and strangely, the fear passed out of me. After a few minutes, I walked back to the motel. When I got to the room, I knocked and said, "Let me in." The door opened. Glass covered the floor. Bob turned and lay down on one of the twin beds, his face to the wall. I entered quietly and began to clean up the mess.

When he finally turned his head to look at me, I said, "That's the last time this will ever happen, the last time you will ever have the chance to do this." I began to separate our clothes in the suitcases. At first he was contrite. For the rest of the night, by turn, he resorted to attacking me verbally, calling me names, then begging me to stay with him. The harangue continued through the following morning. He didn't stop to draw breath until we got into the car with Dad and Cici to go to the airport, and then he fell silent through the flight, until we arrived in Los Angeles. I think he couldn't believe the end had become a reality. I barely could.

I don't know if I would have had the courage to leave him on my own. Dad was silently in my corner. It seemed unthinkable, but after four roller-coaster years, Bob and I were parting ways. When the suitcases appeared on the carousel, I took mine off. "I'm staying here," I said. "This is goodbye." He extended his hand. "If you were the last person alive, I wouldn't shake it," I said. I turned away to Dad and Cici and walked out of the airport to their car. That was the last time I ever saw Bob Richardson.

Shortly afterward, Dad left to make *The Man Who Would Be King,* in Morocco, with John Foreman producing. I stayed in the Pacific Palisades with Cici. It was like a liberation after being with Bob, like finding out I could breathe on my own.

Bob called every day for some weeks. He wrote letters to Dad, claiming that I had dragged him back into addiction.

The last time we spoke, he told me he was in love and going to be a father again. Then he contradicted himself and said he was drunk and asked if I loved him as much as he loved me. I pleaded with him not to phone me anymore. I asked if he could tell by my voice that he was driving me mad, that staying with him would be the death of me. I begged him to leave me alone. Eventually, to my great relief, the calls became less frequent. Then they stopped. I was unspeakably grateful that Dad never mentioned Bob's name nor made any reference to him. It took Dad being there for me to vanquish that dragon, and I think we both knew it.

CHAPTER 17

Anjelica on Desirée at her ranch in
Three Rivers, California

Los Angeles was a dream that I'd cherished for some time. California symbolized light, warmth, glamour, and freedom, although I knew that I probably was not going to find work as a model, not being in the least the popular idea of a California girl. I nevertheless craved sun, the open space, the beach—the comparatively easy living. I put my old life behind me.

Down a rustic canyon, beside Will Rogers State Historic Park and the polo field off the Sunset Strip, Cici's house was next to a beautiful old garden. It had a trail that led to a grove of mature camellia trees whose petals carpeted the dark mulch underfoot in a symphony of pink. I often wandered there for hours.

I loved Cici's company, her easy laugh, and her ironic asides. She was delightful and irreverent, and said exactly what she thought, which was good if she was on your side. We fell into a happy routine—driving in her candy-apple red Citroën Maserati with the top down, the scent of lemon blossom heavy and sweet on the breeze; sunning ourselves on the back terrace of the house, alongside the succulents. After New York, it was a vision of paradise, and soon my most basic wish was fulfilled—I got a suntan.

There was a row of stables at the base of Cici's driveway. Every day, we would saddle up and ride her horses on the winding yellow dirt trails chiseled into the Santa Monica Mountains, overlooking the vast Pacific coastline, and watch the sun rise like a mandarin, baking the mist from the canyons, the first hummingbirds dipping into the flowering hibiscus.

I was surprised that I felt removed from my recent past, as though I had awakened from a dark dream, and that my own resolve not to have anything more to do with Bob was, after years of uncertainty, steadfast. My only choice was to let go and move forward into a bright but unknown future. As Dad used to say to Tony and me when we were children, "Remember, you can always put your hands in your pockets and walk away."

Well, I had done that. And now I was back up on the horse.

ACKNOWLEDGMENTS

I hope that when inconsistencies, mistakes, and omissions appear on these pages they will not be held too severely against me. I am grateful to all the people whose names I have mentioned in this book, and to those we will meet in the next. I appreciate the time we have spent together and your influence on my life.

I'd like to thank my family, especially my darling sister Allegra, whose own memoir was an inspiration. And Tony, Danny, Matt, Laura, and Jack. And the little ones—Jasper, Rafa, Noah, Stella, Sage, and Mathilda, who make the sun rise.

Special gratitude to the many people who played a part in persuading me to share my story. In particular, Mitch Glazer for championing me all along; Graydon Carter, whose encouragement helped me decide to begin writing; Boaty Boatwright for keeping me under her wings; Lillian Ross for her advice, love, and bolstering emails; Betty Bacall for believing in me since the day I was born; Susan Forristal for the gift of her friendship from our early days of modeling to this day, and forever; Jane and Jimmy Buffett for providing a safe haven where I was able to work on the manuscript; and Joan Buck, who was my best friend at eight years old and remains a sister to this day—thank you for opening your archives, sharing the memories, and keeping me on track.

Very special thanks to my wonderful friends for your kindness, your constancy, and your steadfast support, and for making the world a better place. And to the Lynch family and everyone back home in Ireland, and of course Lizzie Spender and Emily Young.

My appreciation to Paper Mate® for their brilliant Sharpwriter #2, which allowed me to write this book by hand. To Stephen Dane, Terry Richardson, Tim Jenkins, Jaqueth Hutchinson, the Avedon Foundation, Paul Jasmin, my cousin Lynn LaMoine, Robert Fleischauer, and everyone who contributed to the photography on these pages.

Profound gratitude to my fine editor, the wonderful Bill Whitworth, who afforded me some important revelations, and in these few months taught me more about the English language than I ever learned in school. To my publisher, Nan Graham, a woman of boundless energy, focus, and intelligence. And to her team at Scribner—Daniel Burgess, Kara Watson, Tal Goretsky, Erich Hobbing, Katie Rizzo, and Kate Lloyd. To my business manager, Britt Bates, and my lawyer, David Nochimson, for your counsel and friendship all these years. To my agent, Bill Clegg, whose bravery inspired me to be bold. Thanks also to the rest of the team in the WME book department: Tracy Fisher, Cathryn Summerhayes, Shaun Dolan, and Chris Clemans. And to Jaclyn Bashoff, my manager, my friend, my compass.